So You're Cremated ... Now What?

Over One Hundred Creative Ways to Scatter Your Ashes and Some Other Useful Information

Written and Illustrated by

By

Jesse Kalfel

iUniverse, Inc.
New York   Bloomington

So You're Cremated...Now What?
Over One Hundred Creative Ways to Scatter
Your Ashes and Other Useful Information

Inquires should be addressed to
info@crematednowwhat.com
Visit us at www.crematednowwhat.com

Library of Congress Control Number: 2009924786

iUniverse books may be ordered through booksellers or by contacting:

iUniverse
1663 Liberty Drive
Bloomington, IN 47403
www.iuniverse.com
1-800-Authors (1-800-288-4677)

Because of the dynamic nature of the Internet, any Web addresses or links contained in this book may have changed since publication and may no longer be valid.

ISBN: 978-1-4401-2775-5 (pbk)
ISBN: 978-1-4401-2776-2 (cloth)
ISBN: 978-1-4401-2777-9 (ebk)

Printed in the United States of America

iUniverse rev. date: 6/10/2009

For my parents, Joe and Nadja, who taught me about wrestling with the Muses.

Disclaimer

All reasonable measures have been taken to ensure the quality, reliability, and accuracy of the information in this book. This book is intended to provide information only. If you are seeking advice on any matters relating to information in this book or scattering permissions, you should—where appropriate—contact the local or private entity directly with your specific query or seek advice from qualified professional people.

We encourage you to take steps to obtain the most up-to-date information and to confirm the accuracy and reliability of any information you require so as not to violate existing dispersal regulations.

Each page in this book must be read in conjunction with this disclaimer. The material in this book is for informational purposes only and is not intended to provide legal, environmental, or religious guidance with reference to any particular situation. No representations, warranties, or guarantees whatsoever are made as to how accurate, current, complete, reliable, suitable, or applicable to a particular situation any of the material might be. If expert professional assistance is required, the services of a competent professional should be sought. Readers assume all responsibilities and obligations with respect to any decisions or advice made or given as a result of the use of any material.

Contents

Disclaimer. vii

Acknowledgments. xv

Preface. xvii

Introduction xxiii

You've Got Options. 1

   Let's Have an "After You're Gone Reality Check". 2

   Now for Some History 3

   Out with a Fizzle. 5

   Getting Hot Again 6

   Religious Issues: Cremation Is Not for Everybody. 8

   Make Sure Everyone Knows You Want to Be Cremated. . 10

   Before You Turn to Ashes 11

   Cremation and Things Suspicious 11

   Save Some Bucks. 12

   Dos and Don'ts of Viewing 13

   No Room for Things That Go Boom. 14

   Things That Gently Will Rise into the Atmosphere 15

   Let's Be Urnest 16

      Urns for Indoor Use: 17

      Urns for Burial: 17

      Urns for the Outdoors:. 17

      Themed Urns: 18

      Religious Urns:. 18

      Urns for Scattering: 18

Now That You Are Ashes. 18

Over 100 Ways to Scatter Your Earthly Remains. 21

I. Staying Put the Old-Fashioned Way. 21
    1. We Really Dig You. 22
    2. Urn Garden 22
    3. Give Me Shelter. 22
    4. Memorial Garden. 23
    5. Environmentally Friendly Options. 23

II. Staying Put at Home: Outside 25
    6. Thinking Outside the Box 25
    7. Under a Memorial Tree 26
    8. Rock Your World 26
    9. Let's Go Get Stoned. 27
    10. A Wetter Idea. 27
    11. Timing Is Everything 27
    12. Together Forever. 29

III. Staying Put at Home: Inside 31
    13. On Display: The Traditional Urn 31
    14. Good Things Come in Tiny Boxes 31
    15. Nighty-Night and Eternal Rest. 32
    16. Objet d'Art 33
    17. Uncle Scrooge Urns 33

Not Very Traditional Urns. 34
    18. Jock in a Box 34
    19. A Fan on Steroids. 35
    20. Hobby Urns. 35

IV. Leaving Home Forever. 37
    Things to Know Before You Scatter 37
    Some Tips on How to Scatter Ashes. 39
    Techniques for Scattering. 39
    H_2O Is the Way to Go. 41
    21. Splish Splash 41
    22. Hanging with King Neptune 43
    23. Old Man River Keeps on Rollin' Along 44
    24. Cascading Your Way Away. 46

V. Some Lofty Ideas. 49
   25. Ain't No Mountain High Enough 49
   26. Towering Infernos 50
   27. Out with a Bang. 51
   28. The Answer, My Friend, Is Blowing in the Wind 52
   29. Eye of the Storm 53
   30. Around the World in Eighty Days 53
   31. Around the Block in a Couple of Hours. 53
   32. Beam Me Up, Scotty, and You're Halfway to Heaven . .54

VI. At One with the Universe ... and with Others 56
   33. Giving Yourself to Others through Food 56
   34. Really Giving Yourself to Others through Food 57
   35. Quenching Your Thirst for Immortality 58
   36. A More Direct Approach 59

VIII. Mostly Amusing Options 61
   37. Revenge Tastes So Sweet. .61
   38. You Party Animal 62
   39. Life Is a Roller Coaster. 64
   40. Clowning Around 64

IX. Disposable Options 66
   41. Too-Da-Loo and Down the Loo. 66
   42. Sink or Swim 67
   43. Trash Night 67
   44. Fluffy Would Be Happy. 67
   45. A Life Aquatic 68
   46. On the Road Again 69
   47. Recycle Your Soul. 69
   48. Anger Management Once You're Gone. 70

X. Scattering Places. 71
   49. A Snow-White Send-Off 71
   50. Life's a Gamble. 72
   51. School Daze. 74
   52. Church Scatterings. 74
   53. The Chosen People Can't Do This 75
   54. Historic Scatterings 76
   55. Military Scatterings 76

56. Feel the Pain. 77
57. I Love Paris in the Springtime 77
58. America, the Beautiful 79
59. Born in the USA 79
60. Other Very Cool Places 80

XI. Arts, Crafts, and Some Other Precious Ideas 86
61. A Diamond Lasts Forever, and So Will You 86
62. And Then There's Costume Jewelry 87
63. You Were Always a Masterpiece 87
64. Urban Art and Tag You're It 89
65. Lasting in Latex 89
66. Let Your Grandkids Commemorate You. 90
67. 'Tis the Season to Be Jolly 91
68. You Had a Magnetic Personality. 91
69. They'll Be Dyeing for You 92
70. Ashes to Ashes 92
71. For Whom the Bell Tolls 93
72. Praise the Lord. 93

XII. Make Something of Yourself Already 95
73. The Donald 95
74. Not the Donald 95
75. Firming Up Some Other Constructive Ideas 96

XIII. Crunchy Granola Ideas. 98
76. Make a Political Statement. .98
77. Okay, You're Not Political—So Let's Light Up 99
78. Finally Making Scents 100
79. Cleanliness Is Next to Godliness. 100
80. Youth Springs Eternal. 101
81. Rub It In 101
82. X-Rated Suggestions Will Not Be Mentioned in This
Book 102
83. Do Yourself a Flavor. 103

XIV. More Than Fifteen Minutes of Fame. 104
84. Cozy Up with the Famous .104
85. Hard and Hardly Famous. .105
86. Give Your Regards to Broadway 105

XV. Being a Good Sport 107

   87. The People in the Bleachers Will Love You 107

   88. The One That Got Away 108

   89. The Big Dusting. 109

   90. A More Intimate Dusting. 110

   91. Giddy Up. 110

   92. When Powder Meets Powder 111

   93. Bambi Will Hate You, and So Will My Kid 111

   94. Lucky Lanes. 112

   95. Minnesota Fats. 112

   96. A Dimpled Approach. 113

   97. Take a Hike 114

XVI. Leaving It to Chance and to Others 115

   98. A Message in a Bottle. 115

   99. Bag It and Pass It 116

   100. Take a Scenic Route 117

   101. A Test of Character. 118

   102. Let Your Fingers Do the Walking 118

   103. Polar Express Yourself. 118

   104. Highest Bidder. 119

   105. Okay, Just Forget About It 120

APPENDIX A – Sources and Resources 123

APPENDIX B – Flamed and Famous 131

Acknowledgments

To my mother, who gave me the idea for this book when she said she wanted to have her ashes dispersed in four different places. To my first readers, Dave and Jodie Hanson, who thought the book was funny and informative and "would sell like hotcakes." To Drs. Bottner and Carlat, who gave me great suggestions which helped shape the scope and usefulness of this book. And finally to my wife and daughter who supported me throughout this project.

Preface

"I'm not afraid to die. I just don't want to be there when it happens."

--Woody Allen--

You might ask how I decided to write a book like this. I am not a funeral director, nor have I ever had dreams of becoming one (although I was a big fan of the TV show *Six Feet Under*). I am not a grief counselor, although I do occasionally give people grief. The idea simply came from a talk I had with my ninety-seven-year-old mother. At the time of my father's death, my mother, who was in shock as she made funeral arrangements, ordered a single cemetery plot for Dad. I was a teenager at the time and not deeply involved in helping with the plans.

Fast forward thirty-eight years, when my mother sat me down to talk about what she wanted when her time came.

"I could buy a double plot for your father and me," she mused. "But that would be complicated since we would have to unearth your father. I'm sure he is comfortable just where he is. And it would feel strange if I had a separate plot somewhere in the cemetery and not next to him."

"Have you considered cremation?" I asked.

She thought for a while and then nodded. "I like that idea, but I don't want my ashes to be cooped up in an urn."

"I'm sure you have choices about what you might do with your ashes." I said that without really knowing what her choices might be. But then she smiled and started to think out loud.

"Well, you can put a bit of me right over your father's grave," she started. "That way you can visit both of us there. And you know my favorite tree in your backyard? Sprinkle some of me there too. I also want to be scattered over Candlewood Lake, where we spent many lovely summers together as a family."

"I can do that for you," I said.

She patted my hand and said, "Thank you."

It wasn't long after my conversation with my mother that I began asking friends if they had thought about what they wanted to do with themselves once they passed on. I was surprised at how many people said they wanted to be cremated. Some had clear ideas about where they wanted to be scattered, but many said they hadn't figured that out yet. They also mentioned that their parents were thinking of cremation, and what to do with their ashes was still up in the air.

I wondered if there was a book that offered suggestions about scattering, types of urns you can choose, and tips and techniques. I discovered that there were none. I then asked my friends: if they had a book that offered a wide range of suggestions of scattering options and other helpful advice, would they find that valuable? The resounding reply was yes.

I started doing research and began documenting the many commercially available scattering services that are offered. This led me to think of ideas of my own—some playful, some creative, some very unconventional, and some just plain irreverent. Like shoe sizes, one scattering option doesn't fit all.

As I worked on this book, one thought kept remerging. People want to have a say in what kind of funeral they would like. If it's their last production, they want to direct it: who speaks, the kind of service given, what music is played, where it takes place. If cremation is chosen, then how and where they want their ashes scattered is just as important.

* * *

How do you start a book on the many ways and options you have if you decide to scatter your ashes? The subject assumes that you or someone you care about has considered cremation. The thought that our life will eventually have an end is something that most of us would rather postpone thinking about. But our life on earth does come to an end for all of us, and what happens after that is matter of whatever your belief system is.

Maybe there's a heaven, maybe a hell, maybe reincarnation, maybe nothing at all. If there is a heaven, you might be headed there. If you were on Santa's naughty list, you might be headed to a hotter climate. If you have a Buddhist point of view, you might believe you get another chance in your next life. Then, of course, maybe there is nothing after the lights go out. If so, there's nothing to worry about since there will be nothing to worry about.

Putting aside all these possibilities, you still need to ask yourself, "What is the last way I want to be remembered?" – along with the eloquent eulogies that will have people grabbing for wads of Kleenex at your funeral.

Quotable Quotes

"They say such nice things about people at their funerals that it makes me sad to realize that I'm going to miss mine by just a few days."

--Garrison Keillor--

Most of us can agree that once our life spirit leaves our body, what is left is our body—the container we carried around for years, the one that went to school, had friends and maybe a family, went to Disneyland, had a job, and collected a lifetime of experiences, hopefully mostly good.

If you are reading this book, then something about the title probably caught your eye. Maybe you are thinking ahead, deciding that cremation might be an option for you or your loved ones. If cremation is a choice, then the question is "So I have been transformed into ashes; now what should I do with them?"

St. Peter was not a big fan of cremated souls when it came to his dry cleaning bill.

What you can do with your ashes as a final statement is what this book is all about—and there's no other book like it. There are more than a hundred suggestions of ways that you can scatter your ashes. Some are thoughtful, some are funny. Some are truly creative, some are irreverent. What you choose can reflect your personality, a final statement you want to make, or something meaningful that puts you in the director's chair for your final act in the play that was your life.

If cremation is a considered choice, this book provides a way to start thinking and discussing this subject, especially with the ones you love. This is a book that offers some creative ideas, with a few chuckles along the way.

Furthermore, for the first time you have a book that compiles most of the commercially available scattering possibilities in a single volume, along with some of my own suggestions.

For example, did you know that you can disperse your earthly remains by being packed into fireworks, or have them shot into space, placed inside a time capsule, scattered around exotic locales anywhere in the world, turned into a real diamond, or cast into a pink flamingo lawn sculpture? *So You're Cremated ... Now What?* is not a somber how-to manual. It is written with humor in a tongue-in-cheek style that starts out with a little history, then gives you some funeral tips along with cremation dos and don'ts. After that, you can burn through these pages and read some sizzling ideas about what you can do with your ashes—whether scattered, buried, mailed or left outside with the recycling. Some of these ideas will have numbers following them that refer to commercially available services you can make use of, which are listed by number in Appendix A; look for references like this: (12). And for those of you who want to be reassured that other people have chosen cremation, a list of some of our more famous predecessors are listed in Appendix B.

I hope you will benefit from these thought-provoking and entertaining possibilities to help you make a lasting final statement. Happy scatterings!

Did You Know

You will be in good company if you choose cremation. Many famous people already have: Walt Disney, Henry Fonda, Greta Garbo, Tupac Shakur, Dorothy Parker, John Lennon, Albert Einstein, Jerry Garcia, Ingrid Bergman, Isaac Asimov, and Harpo Marx, to name a few.

Introduction

"I am ready to meet my Maker. Whether my Maker is prepared for the great ordeal of meeting me is another matter."

~~Winston Churchill~~

Unless you are a Buddhist and can't wait for reincarnation and another crack at getting your next life right, once you are gone, what happens next is something we can debate until kingdom come.

The one thing everyone can agree on is that we all have bodies, and after we give up the ghost, something has to be done with us to keep the air around the house from getting as funky as an unplugged refrigerator in August.

The upshot is that something has to be done with our package, the body we dragged along to school, parties, the office, and summer vacations. For many, that translates into being laid to rest the old-fashioned way—getting buried. We've been burying ourselves for a lot of years now. Thousands and thousands of years, as it turns out.

Did You Know

According to experts, our Cro-Magnon relations were the first hominids to bury their dead. Mungo Man is the world's first evidence of a human ritual burial, while Mungo Lady represents the first known human cremation. Both were discovered in Australia and are about 40,000 years old.*

* News in Science
(http://www.abc.net.au/science/news/stories/s788032.htm)

Although it isn't clear what rituals went along with these first burials and what beliefs they represented, these rituals might have been the first seeds for our deep-seated human urge to make our passing more significant then simply getting sunk six feet under. For many, remembrance is a a way to gain immortality.

Today, we can take charge and orchestrate how we want to be laid to rest and remembered. Our very own funeral can be the event, maybe the last one, where we can shape that remembrance.

If you are in your forties, fifties, or sixties you are seeing the generation before us—our parents, uncles and aunts—thinning out. Many of our families are reconsidering traditional burials. As for the boomer crowd, we are making funeral choices based on very different ideas from what previous generations might have done.

Did You Know

More than 40 percent of Americans will choose cremation by 2010. According to BoomerHQ.com, there are close to 75 million boomers in the U.S. who represent about 29 percent of the U.S. population. That means over 30 million boomers are likely to choose cremation. (1)*

* These numbers in parentheses refer to resources listed in Appendix A.

As we confront the inevitable, cremation is certainly becoming a hot topic and cool alternative for us. Many of us are thinking more "green," or don't like the idea of being buried in some frosty graveyard, or maybe want to be located in a place that has more significance than a cemetery plot. For others, the scattering of our ashes gives us different ways to make an impressive statement that may be more meaningful than a traditional funeral service. The service and scattering that follows can be more creative, memorable, and evocative—tailored as an individualized ceremony befitting the person who has passed on to the blue firmament.

Not that we have become total control freaks or anything. But a lot of us try not to leave much of our lives to chance. The same thing applies to our death. That's why there has been a big increase in people choosing to preplan their own funeral. Preplanning lets you choose the type of service that best fits your beliefs, and, as with a play, you can be the director as well as the star. You can make plans for your last production in simple or dramatic terms—and prevent your family and friends from doing something truly ludicrous and "not you" for your funeral. Better yet, you can relieve them of the burden as well.

Quotable Quotes

"According to most studies, people's number one fear is public speaking. Number two is death. Death is number two! Does that sound right? This means to the average person, if you go to a funeral, you're better off in the casket than doing the eulogy."

--Jerry Seinfeld--

You've Got Options

We all know that funerals are rites of passage: ceremonies that let people who are still aboveground express the loss of a loved one. It's a ritual and experience you can personalize to express your family's beliefs and traditions. It's a time for family and friends to share in the loss. It can be a time of healing by bringing people together to say goodbye to you. What happens during and after the service is a way to find closure. The beauty of cremation versus burial is that you have a lot more options if you want to make a more personalized affirmation. It's your life, and it's your death, so shouldn't you have the last word?

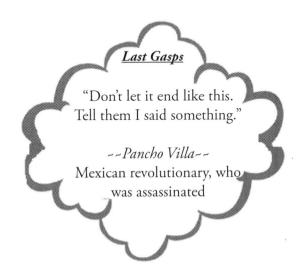

Last Gasps

"Don't let it end like this.
Tell them I said something."

--Pancho Villa--
Mexican revolutionary, who
was assassinated

Let's Have an "After You're Gone Reality Check"

Many people who opt for a burial with a gravestone above their head want a place for their loved ones to visit them. It seems like a nice idea and seems really touching. People can come to a place where they leave flowers, whisper remembrances, maybe apologize for the crummy way they treated you, which is a heck of lot cheaper than therapy.

When it comes to graves, it certainly can help those people you left behind as a place to remember you. However, the fact is that a couple of generations from now the only folks who will make their way to your marker will be the lawnmower guy that you paid for with the Perpetual Care option. Unless you died a real celebrity, you will be as forgotten as all the millions of shooting stars no one ever saw.

Maybe that's hard to believe, so here are a few questions. What is your great-great-great-great grandfather's name, where is he buried, and when was the last time you went to his grave? See my point?

> ### *Did You Know*
>
> *Linda McCartney, wife of Paul of Beatles fame, was scattered in two places: on her family farm in England and on their ranch in Arizona.*

If you still like the idea of a permanent place of residence, you can have your ashes buried in a fixed spot. You can stay put or go anywhere you want. Your ashes can be interred in a cemetery plot, displayed in an urn on top of a mantelpiece, or scattered on private property or at a place that was significant to you.

You also have many options that won't keep you grounded. It's your choice. What do I mean by "more options"? Simply stated, you are virtually free to scatter, consign, shoot, drop, bury, or throw your ashes just about anywhere you want. Your big send-off can be fun or solemn, unique, and more environmentally friendly than an ordinary funeral and in-ground burial. And you don't have to limit yourself to just one scattering choice. You may be crazy enough to go for every suggestion in this book. What's more, you have a rich history behind you, celebrities who have gone before, and some very creative choices ahead of you. (See Appendix B.)

Now for Some History

Who knows when or how cremation started? Maybe it was some caveman with bad hand-eye coordination who was grilling a loin of woolly mammoth. The chunk of woolly slipped off the spit, landed in the fire pit, and burned to a crisp—and an idea was born. Maybe a recently widowed Roman potter decided that he wanted his dear departed wife near him, and what better way to contain her ashes than with something he would call an urn.

When Ooog accidentally dropped the woolly mammoth leg into the fire pit, he sensed his grave-digging days were over.

3

Historians and archeologists tell us that cremation goes back to the Stone Age, and most archeologists point to Europe and the Near East as where the tradition began. By the time the Bronze Age (2500 to 1000 BC) rolled around, cremation made its way to the British Isles and Southern Europe (2) where ashes were typically interred in bronze urns. Those who cling to the idea of resting in a cemetery will be happy to know that the first people who got cremated still wanted folks to drop by and pay their respects. It was the Iberian Celts who established the first cremation cemeteries around 600–450 BC.[1]

Cremation cemeteries started popping up across Europe faster than teenager acne so that people could visit with a jug of wine and a loaf of bread and tell the deceased the latest "why did the Minotaur cross the road" jokes. (Chicken jokes were not invented yet.)

Creative dispersal outside a cemetery would have to wait a while.

When Homer and the Greeks came along in the ninth century BC, cremation was the preferred way to go off to Hades. As early Balkan environmentalists, they promoted the idea for sanitary and health reasons. It was also a good way to tackle the problem of disposing of all those slain soldiers strewn around the battlefields of Troy and other places of carnage. Lack of refrigeration can be a big pain

Not wanting to be left behind, the Romans got on the bandwagon around 500 BC. Cremation was so much the rage that the one of the emperors—an early pollution-control pioneer—had to publish an official decree against cremating bodies within city limits because the smoke was getting thicker than LA smog (3).

---

1 Journal of Interdisciplinary Celtic Studies, Vol. 6.

Out with a Fizzle

They say all good things must come to an end. That's when early Christian and Jews finally put a stop to cremation. The early Christians considered it way too pagan. For Jews, autopsies, wakes, open caskets, embalming, and cremation were all Yahweh no-nos.

"Well, there goes our business!"

The final nail in the coffin was hammered by Emperor Constantine around AD 330, when he Christianized the Roman Empire. Constantine, a pagan who once worshipped the sun, was over forty years old when he finally declared himself a Christian. It is said that his conversion took place just before a battle that would determine who would be the leader of the Roman Empire. He started to pray for help. In a dream he saw Jesus telling him to use the chi-rho sign "as a safeguard in all battles." Constantine ordered it to be put on his soldiers' shields—and miraculously won the battle. [2]

Constantine went back to burying folks the old-fashioned way. In no time at all, being interred in the ground had totally replaced cremation aside from exceptional circumstances like plagues, and that was that.

Did You Know

In Greece, cremation was the custom for everyone except suicides, unteethed children, and persons struck by lightning. The Romans continued the practice to the end of the 4th Christian century, where burning on the pyre or rogus was the general rule. *

* LoveToKnow Classic Encyclopedia

Getting Hot Again

Cremation, as we know it today, was a dead issue for almost 1,700 years. It wasn't until 1873 that two peculiar events took place to put cremation back on the front burner. (4) The first event was an exhibit at the 1873 Vienna Exposition where Professor Brunetti of Italy displayed his very own cremation furnace with the eye-catching cremains of an incinerated body (possibly faked) right next to it.

---

2 Quest Education: request.org.uk/main/history/romans/constantine.htm

Since people have always been drawn to macabre and outlandish things, this exhibit was one of the hottest hits at the fair.

It turns out that one special visitor to the professor's exhibit happened to be Queen Victoria's surgeon, Sir Henry Thompson. Impressed, he was the first person of distinction to recommend the practice for sanitary reasons, since the toxins of the dead were thought to pollute water, ground, and air. Plus, London real estate prices next to cemeteries were really getting slammed.

The second event took place three years later in a small town in Pennsylvania on December 6, 1876. The recently departed Baron Joseph Henry Louis Charles De Palm went up in smoke in an affair presented as the first modern-day cremation in America (5).

Did You Know

*The first preplanned cremation in the United States actually took place about ninety years earlier. Colonel Henry Laurens, a member of General George Washington's staff and president of the Continental Congress, went the toasty way in 1783. Laurens ordered that he be cremated, fearing he would be buried alive. This demand came about after his daughter, who had been stricken by smallpox and was about to be interred, suddenly sprang back to life.** *

---

* Stephen R. Prothero: Purified by Fire: A History of Cremation in America

---

Cremation captured the imagination and attention of Americans as it made it to the tabloids with the baron's inflammatory event. Moreover, religious leaders including Reverend Octavius B. Frothingham, who led a band of ministers and pro-cremationists with sermons that espoused both the spirituality and sanitary science of incineration, added more fuel to the fire of acceptance.

The reaction from the public was split. Some believed that this was the dawn of a new age for burial simplicity. Foes, on the other hand, said it was the work of the devil (fire, after all, is the devil's best friend). But in any case, the baron had lit a fire under the cremation movement.

In no time, crematories—the places where cremations take place—were spreading like wildfire. By 1913, there were over fifty of them operating in cities including New York, Pittsburgh, Buffalo, Cincinnati, Detroit, and Los Angeles.

Nowadays, cremation is a flourishing first choice for many of those who reach the end of the road. According to the Cremation Association of North America, the number of cremations in North America has more than tripled since 1973. Other countries have even higher rates: Japan (97 percent), Great Britain (70 percent), and Scandinavia (65 percent). Today, there are close to 1,500 crematories in the United States with nearly 700,000 cremations performed every year. By 2010, the cremation rate in the US will be close to 40 percent.

Religious Issues: Cremation Is Not for Everybody

People of faith who consider cremation may want to check whether their religion actually approves of the practice, since you wouldn't want to jeopardize entry into a better place in the hereafter.

According to answers.com and the Columbia Electronic Encyclopedia, the following religions permit cremation:

- Baptist
- Buddhist (some believe that the Buddha was cremated, and embrace the practice to follow his example)
- Calvinist
- Christian Scientist
- Christian Churches of England, Scotland, Ireland, and Wales
- Hindu
- Jehovah's Witness

- Liberal Jewish
- Lutheran
- Methodist
- Moravian
- Mormon
- Presbyterian
- Roman Catholic Church
- Salvation Army
- Seventh Day Adventist
- Sikh
- Society of Friends (Quaker)
- Unitarian-Universalist

Did You Know
If you're a Roman Catholic, you can breathe a sigh of relief since the Pope lifted the ban on cremation in 1963 and allowed Catholic priests to officiate at cremation ceremonies. However, you can't be scattered at sea. It seems that when the Second Coming comes, the Big Guy wants whatever is left of you in one package and in one place.

If you practice Greek Orthodox Christianity and live in Greece, you will be thrilled to hear that a law has been recently passed so that you too can be cremated—the result of overcrowded cemeteries. However, if you are Greek Orthodox and happen to live in New Jersey or any other place, you can forget about cremation for now, since special dispensation has not been granted anywhere else. Who said a religion had to be logical?

If you are followers of the following religions, you'd better look for a casket and nice plot to be buried in since cremation is *verboten*: Greek Orthodox Christianity, Islam, Orthodox Judaism, Parsee, Russian Orthodox Christianity, and Zoroastrianism.

If you are an atheist, of course, you won't care. If you are agnostic, you'll have something else to be unsure about.

One other thought to mull over has to do with resurrection, if you have that belief. Some suppose that when resurrection time comes along, God will have trouble resurrecting people from ashes, especially ashes that have been spread. But let's be real here. We're talking about the Big Guy (or Girl), , Who can do anything. Besides, whether you are cremated or buried, you decompose. Your body after death is just a spent container. Your soul has departed.

The only significant difference between the two processes is the time it takes for a body to decompose. Cremation just gets you to dust faster. Neither nature nor the great Almighty will discriminate between how your dust became dust or where it is located. Like the song says that the band Kansas sings:

"Nothing lasts forever but the earth and sky
It slips away
And all your money won't another minute buy
Dust in the wind
All we are is dust in the wind
All we are is dust in the wind"

Make Sure Everyone Knows You Want to Be Cremated

Just because you want to be cremated doesn't make it so. You need to make preparations before you actually check out. And you may have a lot of questions you want answered (6). This lets you create the send-off you really want without the pressure of not having the proper paperwork needed.

The first thing to do is to put your wishes in writing and make it legal. Your family lawyer can help you with that. In many states, you can't authorize your own cremation, so your next of kin must agree.

> *Did You Know*
>
> *According to the Cremation Association of North America, the top states where about half the people who die choose cremation are Hawaii, Washington, Nevada, Alaska, Arizona, Montana, Colorado, Florida, Vermont, Maine, and New Hampshire.*

Better make nice-nice with them before you kick the bucket. Check with your lawyer or funeral home to find out if your state agrees to self-authorization. Also, if you want to be scattered, you should check if there any restrictions regarding where you want to be strewn. If there are, then it's up to you if you want to follow them. At this point, you can't be thrown in jail if you don't follow the rules. However, your scatterers might run a risk. But if they really, really loved you, guilt and whatever you leave them in your will might give them the spunk to get the job done.

Before You Turn to Ashes

Like Buddha, you need to think about what you accumulated in terms of inner wealth. Unlike Buddha, we are talking about internal assets—things like pacemakers, prostheses, and any other mechanical or radioactive devices or implants. As you can imagine, these things go boom when things get really hot for you, if you get my drift. What's more, your estate would be held responsible for any damage caused by exploding gadgets.

Have the people taking care of your last voyage tell the funeral home of any implants. Also let the funeral director know if you were recently treated with any radioactive medication, since we don't want a mini-Chernobyl event to hallmark your last rites. Finally, note that personal possessions or valuable materials that are buried with you, like jewelry or the gold and silver in your teeth, will be ruined, or at the very least melted. And guess who gets to keep that precious puddle? Of course, you could think of it as a generous tip to the funeral staff.

Cremation and Things Suspicious

If your death was untimely or suspicious, don't sweat it (at least not until you get loaded into the chamber). If your death looks "funny," chances are officials will perform an autopsy to determine that someone isn't getting away with murder. Here is how the coroner's office in Yolo County, California, puts it:

> The Coroner is required by state law (G.C. 27491) to investigate all unnatural deaths or deaths where the attending Medical Doctor is unable to state a cause of death as well as cases where the deceased has not been seen by a doctor for 20 days prior to death. It is the responsibility of the Coroner's Office to establish positive identity of the deceased; determine the place, date and time; and the cause and classification of death. The Coroner's investigation is not limited to the examination of the deceased, but may include interviews with family members and other witnesses, the collection of physical evidence and the safeguarding of personal property found at the death scene. (7)

On an unrelated topic, make sure someone identifies you before cremation takes place. You want to be sure it's really you there at the memorial service that people are eulogizing, blubbering wildly about, and hoping they're in your will.

Save Some Bucks

Many people who choose cremation can't stand the idea of paying lots of bucks for an event they won't get to see. According to the U.S. Federal Trade Commission, "A traditional funeral, including a casket and vault, costs about $6,000, although 'extras' like flowers, obituary notices,

---

Did You Know

In the 1800s, the local funeral director typically operated a furniture store and built caskets too. In the late 19th century, casket making developed as an industry. Through the early 1950s there were more than 700 casket manufacturers in the United States. Today, there are less than 200. Cremation is one reason for the decline.*

* The Casket and Funeral Supply Association of America

---

acknowledgment cards, or limousines can add thousands of dollars to the bottom line. However, many funerals run a lot more than that, getting closer to $15,000, and that doesn't include the cost of burial." (8)

By comparison, cremation costs can range from just around $800 for a very simple, no-frills cremation to about $2,800 for an impressive funeral with all the works.

When you look at traditional caskets that can go for over $4,000, like those solid mahogany ones with chubby cherubs carved on the panels, you might advise your loved ones to lose the idea that spending money on your funeral is a sign of how much they loved you. In contrast, most funeral homes simply require you to be cremated in a combustible, leakproof, covered container.

Depending on the funeral home, you may be able to rent a fancy casket and tux or dressy outfit if you intend on having an open casket. After the services are over and the casket and outfit are returned, you can hotfoot it over to the crematory, placed in a simple cardboard box.

Dos and Don'ts of Viewing

If you've decided on an open casket, you don't need to be embalmed, which is another way to save some money. It's an extra and unnecessary expense. More important, if you are environmentally concerned, you don't need to poison the air or ground with toxic fluids.

Many people choose cremation for that reason: to be "green" about their burial choice. As an alternative to minimizing any offensive odors while people are saying their last goodbyes, you can be bathed in a fragrant herbal wash. Your casket can be lined with fragrant flowers and you can be splashed with your favorite aftershave or perfume. Or you may think of it as a way to get rid of all the dreadful colognes or perfumes you never liked but always got on your birthday and holidays.

No Room for Things That Go Boom

You or your designated funeral organizers need to make your visitors and loved ones aware of what they may and may not place in your casket. Your people will be held accountable for any injury to funeral staff for which they are responsible. That said, instruct visitors as follows:

- If you were an avid hunter or law enforcement officer, don't have your pals drop in live ammunition or your favorite load. Guess what? They explode during cremation.
- If you were a veteran, ask your buddies not to put souvenir hand grenades into your casket.
- Were you fond of the drink? Let's not have your brewskie brethren toss in little nips, Budweiser cans, or bottles of Merlot.
- Your hobby as a hoopster or tennis player doesn't require these bouncing balls to be deposited with you.
- Had a career in demolition, pest extermination, nuclear science, or asbestos installation? You get the picture.
- If you worked at a toxic waste dump, tell your colleagues not to throw in any memorial sludge.

Things That Gently Will Rise into the Atmosphere

Anything that will burn without explosion or produce a toxic cloud can be slipped into your casket or container when you are cremated. Here are some ideas:

- Flowers and dried plants are pretty safe, except for that funny stuff you used to smoke. Leave that in your will for the kids.
- Photographs, especially the compromising ones where you are topless on that Club Med vacation or the one with Brandy doing that lap dance thing at cousin Louie's bachelor party.
- Embarrassing love letters to or from people other than your spouse.
- Your little black book, since you won't need it now.
- Those sex toys you hid from the kids.
- Any other scandalous ephemera including diaries, unless you happen to be a renowned literary luminary, Hollywood celebrity, public servant, or soon-to-be historical figure and need to preserve background material for your tell-all biography.
- Every rejection letter you ever received from girlfriends, boyfriends, prospective employers, and publishers, if you saved them for some pathetic reason.
- All those worthless stock certificates you owned after the dot-com bubble burst.
- That terrible first novel you wrote, along with those whiny poems from high school.
- That speech you should have given that could have changed the course of the world.
- Your last will and testament—to really infuriate your family.
- Your lifetime season tickets to a major-league sports team, to piss off that brother-in-law you never liked.
- A few *Playboy* or *Playgirl* magazines, since you don't know what kind of sex you can expect in the hereafter.
- Ashes of your pets, since chances are no one else will want them once you are gone.

Did You Know

Many pet owners are turning to the nation's nearly 700 pet cemeteries to give their animal companions a proper farewell. A grieving pet parent can choose from a range of services including cremation, in-ground burial, or placement in a pet mausoleum.*

* foxnews.com

Let's Be Urnest

Now it's time to take a look at cremation urns, which many people choose to hold their venerated remains. An urn can be personalized and provide an everlasting memorial to celebrate the life of one who is heading to that glorious gate at the end of the sky.

Urns come in all shapes and sizes, from a traditional bronze model resembling an oversized incense burner to a highly decorative frou-frou number that might look really swell on Elton John's piano. Actually, the choices can be quite mind-boggling. But with some guidance from an expert, you can select the perfect urn. Unfortunately, you may have a hard time finding anyone listed in the Yellow Pages under "urn experts," so let's try giving you a little advice right now.

First, you need to decide what's to be done with the urn and you. For example, if you want your ashes to be scattered at sea, a biodegradable urn would be an appropriate choice (unless you want to linger on

Did You Know

One of the most unusual urns ever made was the infamous cookie jar urn. It is housed in the San Francisco Columbarium, the largest repository for ashes in the western U.S. It survived both the 1906 earthquake and the 1937 ordinance outlawing cemeteries. The copper dome, looming over 3 acres of gardens, encloses inlaid marble floors, stained glass windows, tiered circular balconies and ceiling mosaics.*

* www.findagrave.com

the bottom of the ocean in a metal urn like the rusting hulk of the *Andrea Doria*).

On the other hand, if your urn is to be the centerpiece of an outdoor memorial, then consider something durable that will withstand rain, sleet, snow, and occasional bird droppings. If you want to be situated inside your home, then think carefully about the kind of vessel in which you want to be deposited. Keep in mind that you have many choices, all of which are bona fide options.

Let's start thinking about what kind of urn suits you by associating the type of urn with where you would like to be placed. (9)

Urns for Indoor Use:

Think about what might look nice on a mantelpiece, bookshelf, or china closet. Of course, you could be shoved into the back of a closet, so you better work on being adored by the kids before you pop off.

Urns for Burial:

Think cheap, since no one is going to see this urn unless you're dug up by a future archeologist.

Urns for the Outdoors:

Think lawn sculpture, and consider something kitschy if you appreciated tastelessness, like being cast into a pink flamingo or lawn gnome. If you want the respect you never got when alive, think classic sculpture like Rodin's *The Thinker* or something that resembles a statue of a dead president or Civil War general. There are companies that will add your ashes to the sculpture that they cast. More on that later.

Themed Urns:

Do you want to be remembered through an urn that captures your love of golf, horses, or some other hobby besides chasing after someone half your age? If so, a themed urn may be appropriate.

Religious Urns:

Your spiritual commitment and purely led life were no doubt impressive, so how about an urn that wins you some extra points with Saint Peter? Urns crafted like the *Pietà, Praying Hands*, or a cute cherub will reinforce the notion that you were a devout soul.

Urns for Scattering:

Maybe you could rent one of these because, after you are scattered, the only thing it might be good for is a flower vase. Save some money, and you might consider other low-cost types of containers for scattering like a shoebox, mayo jar, or shopping bag.

Now That You Are Ashes

Now it's time to figure out exactly what to do with your ashes. Since this book offers you over a hundred ways to consign your mortal remains, you need to think about **where** and **how** you want to end up. A good place to begin is to decide **where**.

You really have two basic options: ***staying put*** in an identified spot or setting where people can "find" you, or ***having your ashes scattered*** so that you become the cosmic dust that will be absorbed into Mother Nature's life cycle. According to Joseph J. McCabe, president of Everlife Memorials, 68 percent of ashes are kept scattered over water (30 percent), land (20 percent), or at a spot the deceased requested (18 percent). The other 32 percent choose to have their ashes buried in urn burial vaults, or a family member, spouse, or loved one retains the ashes in a keepsake urn.

Again, if you select scattering, always be sure to check local, state, and federal laws. If the location is on private property, you should seek permission of the owner. If it is on public land, you should check local regulations.

Quotable Quotes

"The only thing wrong with immortality is that it tends to go on forever."

~~Herb Caen~~

Over 100 Ways to Scatter Your Earthly Remains

Okay, now we can get to the creative stuff about how you can take care of your ashes. I'm sure there's more than a hundred ways, but this book will give you a good start on what you can do today.

I. Staying Put the Old-Fashioned Way

Maybe you think you'll be lonely and would like the occasional visitor. Or maybe you want to make sure that those you leave behind can be comforted by having a place to find and call on you. Having a permanent spot to stow your ashes, marked with a gravestone or modest monument, gives the living and future generations a place to gather from time to time to visit you, maybe exchange stories about your wild and crazy past, let people mumble little prayers over you, or have a one-sided conversation with you where you'll be forced to be a very good listener.

If one or more of these scenarios strike a chord, then staying put offers several good options—some more traditional and a few with creative alternatives.

So here we go.

1. We Really Dig You

You guessed right, getting buried is the oldest tradition. And where is that but in the old-fashioned cemetery. People can choose to be buried in an urn with a marker as a permanent testimony to having actually lived.

When choosing a cemetery, explore the options for the final placement of urns. Most cemeteries will let you bury your ashes in a traditional grave with an upright or in-ground gravestone or monument. Some cemeteries require an urn vault made of cement to protect the urn from water.

Did You Know

Steve Allen, Lucille Ball, Humphrey Bogart, Walt Disney, W. C. Fields, Marvin Gaye, Burt Lancaster, Michael Landon, and Greta Garbo had their ashes buried in traditional graves.

---

2. Urn Garden

There's another option for those of you who want to be in a cemetery so folks can find you. A good number of cemeteries have special urn gardens for the permanent placement and burial of urns. These are smaller grave sites compared to a traditional burial plot. Think of it as an in-ground condominium.

3. Give Me Shelter

Another option is a nice niche in what is called a *columbarium*. A columbarium is usually located inside a building or church and contains what amounts to a wall of cubbyholes for storing urns—kind of like mailboxes at the post office. Many cemeteries offer options like the single niche for one urn, a companion niche that holds up to three urns, and the family niche for eight urns.

> <u>*Did You Know*</u>
>
> *Roman columbariums were large underground vaults where cremains were placed within small wall niches. Many Romans belonged to funeral societies, called collegia, to ensure proper burial. They would pay monthly dues that would be employed to cover the cost of funerals for members. Collegia members in good standing were guaranteed a nice niche in a columbarium.* *
>
> * "Cremation in a Roman Port Town," University of Michigan

4. Memorial Garden

Instead of a cemetery, you may want your church to be your final resting place. Many churches now offer memorial gardens as an option for placing your ashes on their grounds or inside the building.

5. Environmentally Friendly Options

Consider this. Each year, 22,500 cemeteries across the United States bury approximately: (10)

- 827,060 gallons of embalming fluid, which includes formaldehyde
- 30-plus million board feet of hardwoods (caskets)
- 90,272 tons of steel (caskets)
- 14,000 tons of steel (vaults)
- 2,700 tons of copper and bronze (caskets)
- 1,636,000 tons of reinforced concrete (vaults)

If these statistics get your ecological dander up, then you may want to consider a greener way to go. The US isn't the only country dealing with green alternatives. In land-scarce Hong Kong, cremation is more common and affordable than burials. According to the Associated Press, cardboard "eco-coffins" have become really popular at Hong Kong's busy crematoriums since they are more efficient and minimize the toxic gas produced during combustion.

In the US, you can find many nature preserves billed as "alternative" green cemeteries where the customary aspects of a cemetery are nowhere to be found. Instead of manicured lawns, bodies loaded with embalming fluids, or bunker-like vaults, you can be scattered or urned (biodegradable if you want) in a native ecosystem complete with flowing streams, ponds, wildflowers, forests, and occasional sightings of Bambi. These hallowed grounds may have hiking trails and meditation areas that provide serenity and solace. You were an avid environmentalist in life, so why not in death? (11)

Did You Know

If you're in a rural area, the cheapest option might be a burial on your property. Some states leave it up to municipalities to regulate burial, so have your family check laws before they grab a shovel.

II. Staying Put at Home: Outside

The idea of being away from what was familiar is too much to bear, so you would like to be located on your property instead of some cemetery, assuming you actually have some property. As Dorothy so memorably said, "There's no place like home." Here are some ideas for all you homebodies.

6. Thinking Outside the Box

If you have a house with a garden, a yard, or acreage, you can be interred right on your property. You can have your ashes spread directly into your favorite spot: in a flower bed, under a favorite bush, or over that lawn you hated to mow. It'll be someone else's turn to take care of them (and by association, of you). Of course, if the kids sell the house, you may want taking care of you and your spot as part of the purchase and sale agreement.

For urbanites, people without a garden, or tenants in an apartment building—no problem. Your favorite flower pot or window box will do just fine. Add some Miracle-Gro just for insurance.

Did You Know?

Red Barber (the famous sports broadcaster), Bill Bixby (the actor who played on My Favorite Martian and was TV's Incredible Hulk), Bennett Cerf (cofounder of Random House), Ted Cassidy (he was Lurch in the Addams Family), and actor Richard Harris were all scattered on their properties.

---

7. Under a Memorial Tree

Instead of being buried under a grave marker, consider having your ashes buried in your yard under a tree planted of your choosing. Weeping willows are an obvious choice, but a nice fruit tree would also do nicely, especially if your ashes are mixed in with fertilizer when the tree is first planted. Think about all those people who will truly become one with you when they eat those tasty fruits at harvest time. You'll be eternally yummy in someone's tummy.

8. Rock Your World

If burying your ashes around your property willy-nilly doesn't grab you, and you prefer more permanence, why not be buried inside a memorial boulder (or even a realistic bark-encrusted tree stump). These rocks, which can come in a variety of shapes and sizes, hold your cremated remains in a special waterproof container within the cast stone. Kind of like being entombed like mighty Pharaoh right outside your own home. (12)

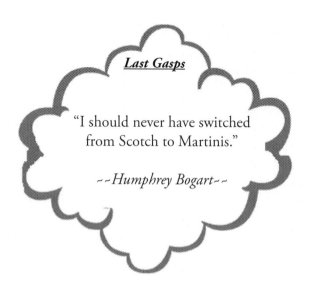

Last Gasps

"I should never have switched from Scotch to Martinis."

--*Humphrey Bogart*--

9. Let's Go Get Stoned

If you're concerned that you'd be taken for granite with your ashes inside a rock, then consider mixing your ashes into cast stone to create a beautiful sculpture for display in your home or outside in the garden. Think of the possibilities: a six-foot pink flamingo, a serene Buddha, a leprechaun, a birdbath, a giant bottle of Johnny Walker, or a statue of you looking like Julius Caesar before Brutus whacked him. In time, you might even have a lovely patina of lichen covering you for a truly rustic look. (13)

Pedro always had an affinity to flamingoes.

10. A Wetter Idea

Given all those donations you sent to the Sierra Club and Save the Three-Toed Sloth, you might want to consider another outdoorsy theme: you can be cast into rock-panel cliffs for a prefabricated waterfall right in your backyard. (14)

11. Timing Is Everything

How about staying put, but with the idea you will be discovered some time in the distant future. If you like this idea, then it makes perfect sense that you want whoever or whatever exists on our planet a hundred years, a thousand years, or even a million years from now to know that you lived a special life. Picture an archaeologist, or even an alien, unearthing a time capsule buried on your property or some other location with you and your stuff inside. You might be a real sensation like when they found King Tut's tomb. Guaranteed, these future beings will study your remains and anything else you place in the time capsule as a remarkable portal into the past—your past. Aside from your ashes, you can add other items inside the custom-built container to protect your items from the ravages of time, moisture, and urban renewal. (15) How about these:

- Everyday items you had to have that are common today, but may be obsolete in the future
- DVDs of your favorite movies, songs, and TV series to show people of the future what bad taste really means
- The *Encyclopaedia Britannica* on a CD to show folks how much we didn't know
- Photos of you, your family, and friends to demonstrate what a funny-looking race of people we were
- Home movies and recordings of your voice so that anthropologists of the future can laugh at the primitive rites of you and your ancestors
- Sample of your DNA so you can be resurrected (don't count on it if they see your photos and home movies)
- Seeds of your favorite fruits and vegetables to reveal why we had so much gas
- A key and a made-up treasure map to really frustrate whoever finds you
- A sampling of junk mail, copies of *Reader's Digest*, State of the Union addresses, and Dear Abby columns to demonstrate our advanced culture
- The Bible, Koran, Buddhist scripture, and the four Vedas of Hinduism. Let the people of the future figure out if there really is intelligent design, a God, evolution and what exactly happened to that soul of yours that was attached to your ashes

Where you place or bury your time capsule should also be considered and whether you want to leave future instructions as to its location. You may also choose to leave it up to chance and let fate take its course as to when or whether you will be discovered.

Quotable Quotes

"If the doctor told me I had only six minutes to live, I'd type a little faster."

~~Isaac Asimov~~
(1920–1992)

---

12. Together Forever

How about doing a group thing? Do you have a lot of friends? Do they all want to be cremated and like you are a cultured group that loves art, a beautiful spot on a commanding hill, and outdoor sculpture? If you have answered yes to all of the above, then you need to form the "Together Forever Burial Society" (although any name will do).

Here's how it works. Get at least ten friends—or the more the merrier—to join your burial society. Next, get a reputable law firm that will be in existence at least fifty years from now. After that, have a meeting with a sculptor you all admire, and have him or her design a beautiful outdoor sculpture that can be placed on a piece of land that your group just loves. Buy that land. Have the sculpture created and along with it a mold of the piece since the sculpture will be made of cast stone that can be poured into the mold.

As each of your society members die and are cremated, their ashes will be stored and "managed" by the law firm in some safe location. When the last of your members dies and their ashes are delivered to the firm, bring in a company that makes cast stone goop, and have every burial member's ashes mixed into the goop, which will then be poured into the sculpture's mold.

Once the casting is set and dry, your sculpture can be placed on that pastoral spot you all selected years before. Think of it—all of you, together again, and a work of art to boot! (16)

Did You Know

Want an urn that's a three-dimensional bust of you with your ashes packed inside so you can stare down at those still breathing? Look no more! Check out zornex.com, which will make an exact replica of your head, with facial details including eyes, ears, nose, mouth, and even moles. The bust is attached to a granite base that holds your cremains to form your personal everlasting pyramid. Moreover, the Nevada-based company creates Personal (DNA) Genome Vaults, preserving the loved one's genetic strands inside the pyramid with the three-D memorial bust mounted on top of it. Go to www.zornex.com/zyberi/

The Together Forever Burial Society always thought of themselves as serious thinkers.

III. Staying Put at Home: Inside

Maybe the idea of being smooshed into your garden soil, put under a rock, or transformed into a lawn ornament is too outdoorsy for you, what with cold winters, hot summers, and acid rain. You want shelter, the comforts of home, and some human contact so that someone can brush a little dust off your urn once in a while. Let's see what you can do if this appeals to your stay-at-home sensibilities.

13. On Display: The Traditional Urn

Perhaps you like the idea of being memorialized and placed in a warm, cozy room. You want to be a constant reminder and possible eyesore to your bereaved family and friends. Mostly, you would love to hear what people say about you now that you are gone. The answer is simple: have your ashes put into an urn and placed on your mantelpiece. If there's no mantelpiece, any lamp table, china cabinet, or bookshelf will do. Urns, as you will soon see, come in all sorts of shapes, sizes, materials, and themes. (17).

Alternatively, you could be on display but still making a statement. You never went for the conventional in life, so why should you now that you've left town for good? Forget about those boring urns that look like cast-iron sports trophies from Queen Victoria's time. How about something different? There are lots of possibilities to explore, and we can hardly exhaust them here. Think of these as jumping-off points for your own considerations.

14. Good Things Come in Tiny Boxes

Wood is a good choice if you want something warmer with grain. You can actually have urns made that look like tiny coffins, something that Barbie and Ken Funeral Directors might have in their dollhouse. You can even have these handmade natural oak boxes come with your photo, name, and birth/death dates laser-engraved directly into the wood.

31

Let's hope that the photo you picked out is flattering and not the one from the very last party you attended when you got food poisoning from the sushi and abruptly expired. (18)

15. Nighty-Night and Eternal Rest

People knew you as a late sleeper who loved to pull the covers over your head and slumber till noon. That's why a fabric-wrapped urn is just for you—so you can get your eternal rest in an urn that has a comfortable pillow feel to it. These cozy containers are satin-lined with a fleece center and then covered in silk. Better yet, they are easy to carry if anyone wants to take you on a sleepover or on that around-the-world tour you never got to take in life. (19)

Effie Jean Robinson
Come blooming youths, as you pass by,
And on these lines do cast an eye.
As you are now, so once was I;
As I am now, so must you be;
Prepare for death and follow me.

Author's Note

*The above epitaph is fairly serious,
but underneath,
someone had added the following:*

To follow you
I am not content,
How do I know
Which way you went.

16. Objet d'Art

Perhaps you want to be remembered as an art lover and patron. Your tasteful urn can make sure everyone knows that. There are companies that will place your ashes into a mold cast with molten glass or bronze. Choose a mold that reflects the artist or piece you liked the most. How about Michelangelo's *David*, the *Venus de Milo*, Rodin's *Thinker*, or something by Picasso or Henry Moore? You could also choose to be a paperweight, something actually useful. (20)

17. Uncle Scrooge Urns

On the other hand, forget about all those fancy-schmancy urns we just described. Save that money, and use it for a really first-rate wake instead. In its place you might choose any of the following no-cost vessels you can find around the house:

- Mayonnaise, peanut butter, or grape jelly jar (must have lid)
- Shoe box
- Cookie jar
- Coffee can
- Tupperware container
- Your favorite soda or liquor bottle (requires a funnel and cork)
- Potato salad tub from the deli
- Ziploc baggie
- Brown paper bag (earth-friendly and biodegradable too)

Did You Know

Fredric Baur, who invented the Pringles potato chip can, was buried in one. Relatives honored his last wish and buried part of his cremated remains in a Pringles can.

"That's not peanut butter dear, that's Grandma Gert."

Not Very Traditional Urns

If the urn options just mentioned still don't resonate with you and how you see yourself, how about an urn that really says something about you and what you loved? Here are some ideas about commercially manufactured theme urns.

18. Jock in a Box

You loved sports, either playing them or watching them. You can have your ashes stowed inside urns shaped like golf bags, baseball bats, footballs, pool tables, and bowling or soccer balls. Were you a rodeo groupie? Then how about being stashed inside an urn shaped like a pair of cowboy boots? However, if you were an avid tiddlywinks fan, that could be a problem. (21)

19. A Fan on Steroids

Everybody who knew you knew that you were more than just a sports fan. You were a fanatic. You watched every game, got more autographs than a fan at a *Star Wars* convention, wore the rally cap, cried when they lost, cried when they won. What better way of storing yourself away forever than inside a game-winning ball (tennis, baseball, football, basketball, ping-pong, even a bowling pin). Just find a reputable sports memorabilia shop, buy the ball you want, and then have someone drill a hole to pour your ashes inside. After that, donate it to the appropriate Hall of Fame. Or bequeath it to your college or high school where it will be forever on display in a nice glass case by the gym or girls' (or boys') locker room.

Did You Know

Not wanting to be placed inside an urn, Meat Loaf, American rock singer, recently revealed that he wants to rest in peace at Yankee Stadium, where he has made arrangements for his ashes to be scattered all over the playing field. Meat Loaf's last wish allows him to always be close to his favorite sports giants. According to Starpulse, he said, "I'm going to be cremated, and a helicopter will drop my ashes over the Yankee Stadium in the Bronx, New York City. I can't tell you which company agreed to do it though, as it's illegal."*

* www.allheadlinenews.com

---

20. Hobby Urns

Are you the type who spent half your life trying to bring back your best memories as a kid through the hobbies you spent hours playing? What about doing some hobby homage by getting an urn made that looks like that old Lionel train, the doll or stuffed animal you loved most, a replica of GI Joe, or one of the superheroes? Better yet, your urn could be a collectible one day that someone would actually keep and display. (22)

Hank always thought of himself as a Supersized hero.

IV. Leaving Home Forever

An urn remaining at home may seem like a dead end with no place to go. Even a scattering around your property may seem too confining. You want to get your essential essence out there into the real world, have a final adventure, a last fling, and make a bigger, more unforgettable statement.

So take your ashes on a journey, scatter or place them somewhere that makes your last wish more memorable, personally significant, poetic, silly, or imaginative. If scattering is in your future, then you'll need to consider a few things first.

Did You Know
The great American composer Aaron Copland had his ashes scattered around the grounds of Tanglewood Music Center where many of his pieces were performed. Jay Silverheels, who played the Lone Ranger's sidekick Tonto, was scattered on the Six Nations Reservation, in Brantford, Canada, where he was born.

Things to Know Before You Scatter

Most laws that apply to funerals are based on public health requirements. The good news is that once you are cremated, there are no public health issues. Extreme heat has a way of eliminating germs.

However, as noted earlier, you might have to deal with state or local laws regarding the scattering of your ashes, especially on public grounds. No state law allows your ashes to be scattered on private property without the consent of the property owner. Check with your local officials and see if you need any permissions or certificates since laws concerning ash scattering differ in each state. Obviously, many people scatter ashes without asking for permission, using the "don't ask, don't tell" approach. Many national and state parks have permit requirements and sometimes location limitations for the scattering of remains. Many cemeteries also have regulations that must be observed.

If you decide to scatter your ashes, you first need to think about the location. As they say in the real estate biz, location is everything. If you are concerned about the memorial aspect and want a place that people can visit, you probably don't want a spot that might get developed into a future shopping mall or a Freddy's Fat Boy Restaurant.

Regardless of the setting you select, a scattering can create an opportunity to make a connection with nature, whether on a mountainside, in a forest or meadow, at sea, or in a nudist camp. Legends abound of people who have had their ashes scattered in places as disparate as a secluded beach on Fuji or, as one devoted Boston Red Sox fan requested, near the Green Monster outfield wall.

Scatterings have also taken on more imaginative forms, which are supported by commercial firms who offer a variety of established services to disperse your ashes (see Appendix A). You will also find on these pages other options—all of them creative, many unconventional, and some that will require work and daring on your part to realize. The options that are not commercially unavailable are my contributions to this book. It won't be hard to figure out which ones they are.

The hockey team wondered if they picked the best spot for John's cremation.

Some Tips on How to Scatter Ashes

Before you scatter, you should know that there are several scattering techniques that are linked with the way you decide to disperse your ashes. Many people envision going to a beautiful spot and simply scattering your loved one's ashes. This can be a beautiful ceremony but scattering ashes has to be done the "right" way.

The word "ashes" evokes the sense of lightness as in "as light as ash." The truth is that your ashes are bone fragments that have been ground down. They normally don't gently flow into the air. That being said, there is a portion of ash that can blow in the wind. Therefore, when scattering ashes, make sure to check the wind direction so they don't blow back in people's faces or onto a boat or wherever you decide to cast your treasured loved one.

Techniques for Scattering

Scattering techniques will vary depending on where and how you decide to be scattered. Here are some terms and associated methods to consider[3]:

> **Casting** is where the ashes are tossed into the wind. Check the direction of the wind, and cast the ashes downwind. Most of the ashes will fall to the ground, and some of the lighter particles will blow into the wind, forming a whitish grey cloud. One person in the group may cast all the ashes or scatter some and hand the container to the next person so everyone has a chance to ceremonially cast the ashes. Another option has people given paper cups or casting cups, which they cast simultaneously in a sort of toasting gesture.

---

3 Scattering techniques described here were taken as excerpts by Mary Hickey—Next Generation Memorials

Trenching is digging a hole or trench in the ground or sand. Then the ashes are placed either directly into the trench or in a biodegradable bag or urn. At the end of the ceremony, friends and relatives can rake over the trench. If done at the beach, it can be timed so that the tide comes in and ceremoniously washes you out to sea.

The blowback from Lowell's ashes cost his family an extra $1045 in dry cleaning expenses.

Raking involves pouring the cremated remains from an urn evenly on loose soil and then raking them into the ground at the conclusion of the ceremony. It is important, once again due to the wind, to keep the urn close to the ground when pouring out the remains. Friends and relatives can take turns raking the ashes back into the earth. This is how they perform the scattering at a scattering garden.

Green Burial is done either at a "Green Cemetery" or at a traditional cemetery. Often cemeteries will allow you to place a biodegradable bag or biodegradable urn at a gravesite of a family member who is already buried as long as the ashes or urn are buried. Check with the cemetery to see what their requirements are.

Water Scattering involves placing the ashes into a body of water. A biodegradable bag or urn is recommended. If you decide to scatter the ashes instead of dropping the urn directly into the water, once again beware of blowback into your gathering. There are also urns on the market designed to gently float away and then quickly biodegrade into the water.

Air Scattering is best carried out by professional pilots and air services that specialize in aerial dispersal of ashes. Some companies will arrange for family and friends to be on the ground watching as the plane flies over where a plume of ashes can be seen from the ground. If friends and relatives are not present, these services can provide the specific time and date of the aerial scattering. Some companies allow close family and friends to fly along.

H₂0 Is the Way to Go

What do Jerry Garcia, L. Ron Hubbard, and Janis Joplin all have in common? What about Ingrid Bergman, Fatty Arbuckle, Rock Hudson, and John F. Kennedy Jr.? They were all buried at sea.

Many people choose to be scattered on water or underneath. Moreover, water has been long regarded as a purifying agent (along with fire—go figure). Think Christian baptism, the Hindu Ganges, Islamic *tahara*, and the Jewish *mikvah*. Let's take a look at some traditional and not-so-traditional ways you can get dunked.

Did You Know

Freddie Mercury from the band Queen was scattered on Lake Geneva, Switzerland.

---

21. Splish Splash

We all came from the sea, so why not return to the sea? Water has great symbolism in most religions. Water is used for cleansing and to restore or maintain a state of ritual purity. Of course, the biggest use of purification by water was when an angry God unleashed the Great Flood and destroyed all humanity, except for Noah and his family, along with pairs of each animal—all doing a time-share on the ark.

Burial at sea, ocean, swamp, lake, or pond can provide that final sanctuary for you. You can be scattered over the frothy surface of just about any ocean or body of water. A GPS system can mark the exact spot so your friends and family can motor out and say hello anytime they want, except during hurricane season. Your ashes can be dropped into the water—plunging to the bottom in an urn—scattered by a plane flying over your selected body of water, sprinkled by hand, or ferried out to your special fishing spot by boat. (23)

If you are going to be scattered over the ocean or a bay, why not hand everyone a fishing pole and a brewski for the trip back so you can cheer up what will be a truly sad event. If you want to be really cool, have some of your ashes drilled and sealed into the handles of your fishing rods. Let these special guests keep the rods.

Here are some additional facts that you may want to consider if you decide to deep-six your urn to the bottom of the ocean where mermaids, Neptune, and Moby Dick's mother-in-law await.

If your goal is sink the urn as deep as possible, here are some depth measurements to mull over:

> #1 Pacific Ocean (35,837 ft) (10,924 meters)
> #2 Atlantic Ocean (30,246 ft) (9,219 meters)
> #3 Indian Ocean (24,460 ft) (7,455 meters)
> #4 Caribbean Sea (22,788 ft) (6,946 meters)
> #5 Arctic Ocean (18,456 ft) (5,625 meters)
> #6 South China Sea (16,456 ft) (5,016 meters)
> #7 Bering Sea (15,659 ft) (4,773 meters)
> #8 Mediterranean Sea (15,197 ft) (4,632 meters)
> #9 Gulf of Mexico (12,425 ft) (3,787 meters)
> #10 Japan Sea (12,276 ft) (3,742 meters)

If your goal is to be poured from the urn and strewn over the widest surface, then here is a breakdown by surface area:

#1 Pacific (155,557,000 sq km)
#2 Atlantic (76,762,000 sq km)
#3 Indian (68,556,000 sq km)
#4 Southern (20,327,000 sq km)
#5 Arctic (14,056,000 sq km)

Did You Know

Actors Bud Abbott (of Abbott and Costello fame), Fatty Arbuckle, Ward Bond (actor from the TV series Wagon Train), Joan Caulfield, William Holden, DeForest Kelley (Star Trek's Dr. McCoy), Janis Joplin, and Peter Lawford were all scattered over the Pacific Ocean.

President Barack Obama paid his last respects to his grandmother, Madelyn Payne Dunham, who helped raise him, before scattering her ashes along a Hawaiian shoreline. Obama scattered the ashes of his mother, Stanley Ann Dunham, at the same location after she died of cancer at the age of 53.

---

22. Hanging with King Neptune

If you love the sea and care about its ecosystem and don't want to be scattered or sunk, then how about turning yourself into part of a complete living reef system? Your memorial reef is a cast concrete structure containing your ashes, and once placed, you can become a new home and habitat for fishies and all types of sea life. For people who choose cremation, eternal reefs offer a choice that replaces cremation urns and ash scattering with a permanent, ecologically caring alternative. Besides, didn't you secretly cherish the Little Mermaid and Nemo? (24)

"There's something about this reef that just turns me on."

<u>Did You Know</u>

Participating members in the Neptune Memorial Reef Project can memorialize themselves in a living reef by placing loved ones' keepsakes or cremated remains into the concrete structures that form the reef. The Neptune Reef consists of 2,000 tons of concrete, in the shape of columns, lentils, statues and arches. Go to nmreef.com for information.

---

23. Old Man River Keeps on Rollin' Along

Perhaps you like the water motif, but the thought of being scattered on the ocean makes you a bit seasick. Then try thinking about pitching yourself into a river, which has a certain appeal because you will be flow, flowing along—kind of like life.

If you want a sacred river, try one of the holy rivers in India: Ganges, Yamuna, Godawari, Narmada, Kaveri, or Sindhu. The Ganges, although holy to Hindus, is also considered the dirtiest river in the world with all those other ashes clogging the waterway. But you're dead, so why should you care? You may even want to convert to Hinduism, since, according to the Hindus, not only man, but even the meanest creatures like insects get liberated and achieve salvation. Face it, you need all the help you can get. Maybe the Ganges, converting to Hinduism, and flying your ashes to India is giving you tandoori-like heartburn nightmares. Here is a list of some of the most famous rivers in the world you can get cast into that are not in India:

- *Danube* (for waltz fans). The Danube flows from Germany through Austria, Slovakia, Hungary, Croatia, Serbia, Bulgaria, and Romania.

- *Missouri* (longest in the USA). The Missouri River flows from Montana into North Dakota, South Dakota, Nebraska, Iowa, and Missouri where it joins the Mississippi River.

- *Mississippi* (for Tom Sawyer fans). The Mississippi runs through two states—Minnesota and Louisiana—and winds alongside Wisconsin, Iowa, Illinois, Missouri, Kentucky, Arkansas, Tennessee, and Mississippi—before pouring into the Gulf of Mexico about 100 miles from New Orleans.

- *Yangtze* (longest in Asia and third-longest in the world). Originating in the Dangla mountains in the eastern part of the Tibetan plateau, the Yangtze flows into the East China Sea near Shanghai.

- *Nile* (longest in the world). With its source at Lake Victoria, the Nile (which is made up of the White Nile and Blue Nile) flows through seven nations to the Mediterranean Sea. The Blue Nile comes out in the mountains of Ethiopia and joins the White Nile at Khartoum, which is the capital of Sudan.

- **Hudson** (if you love New York City). Flowing from the Adirondack Mountains in New York State, the Hudson River empties into the Atlantic Ocean between the tip of Manhattan Island and New Jersey.

- **Jordan** (Jesus took a dip or two here). Running through Jordan, Israel, and Syria, the Jordan River empties into the Dead Sea (now how's that for a great place for your final destination).

- **Amazon** (longest in South America and second in the world). With its source in the Andes Mountains of Peru, the Amazon and its tributaries flow through Peru, Bolivia, Venezuela, Colombia, Ecuador, and Brazil before emptying into the Atlantic.

- **Thames** (your royal pain in the ashes will wash ashore at Windsor castle). The Thames River flows through southern England, passing through London and emptying into the North Sea.

Did You Know

Both Charles Mingus, the jazz great, and George Harrison of Beatles fame had their ashes scattered in the Ganges River in India. George Sanders, the acerbic British actor who committed suicide, had his ashes scattered in the English Channel. Then there's Kurt Cobain—lead singer of American grunge band Nirvana—whose ashes were scattered in the Wishkah River.

---

24. Cascading Your Way Away

You considered the suggestions I've been making about being scattered at sea, on a lake, or even in a swimming pool, but still are looking for a different waterlogged option since nothing has clicked. How about having your ashes plummet off a waterfall where you can get thoroughly churned at the end of the ride? There aren't many unsightly waterfalls in the world, so giving you the ten best is just one person's opinion (and not really mine—go to travelersdigest.com).

- **Gullfoss** (Iceland). Gullfoss is the largest waterfall in Europe.

- **Nachi Falls** (Japan). One of forty-eight separate waterfalls dotting across Mount Nachi, from which you can see the Pacific Ocean.

- **Giessbach Waterfalls** (Switzerland). You'll find these falls in a region filled with crystal-clear lakes, snow-capped peaks, and off-key yodelers.

- **Upside Down Falls** (Oahu, Hawaii). Give your ashes that carbonated feeling when you climb to the summit of Mount Konahuanui, and the water flowing off Upside Down Falls plunges just a few feet before prevailing trade winds blow it back up.

- **Angel Falls** (Venezuela). Hope you never had vertigo since, at nearly 2,700 feet, Angel Falls is the world's tallest.

- **Niagara Falls** (Canada/USA). Just think how entertaining your send-off ceremony can be for all those lovesick honeymooners.

- **Ahuii Waterfall** (Nuku Hiva, French Polynesia). Charles Darwin visited this place, and so did one season of *Survivor*.

- **Victoria Falls** (Zimbabwe/Zambia). A ceremony with your ashes strewn across these falls' mile-long breadth may have to compete with white-water rafters, bungee jumpers, and safari tours.

- ***Iguazu Falls*** (Argentina). Grab onto your heavenly seatbelt as your ashes bump over 275 separate cascades and waterfalls that span 2.5 miles and plunge 269 feet into the Iguazu River.

- If you want a reverse waterfall, there is always the ***Old Faithful Geyser.***

The newlyweds were puzzled by what they saw when they visited Niagara Falls.

V. Some Lofty Ideas

Maybe the water thing actually scared you. You hated swimming in chlorine pools, lakes with sunfish that nibbled your knees, and those big ocean waves that knocked you over and pushed sand inside your bathing suit. Maybe you need to replace water-scattering ideas with higher and more heaven-bound ambitions.

25. Ain't No Mountain High Enough

You always liked a room with a view. What's different now? How about a mountain, one of those really tall ones, where not only do you have terrific panoramic vistas but you are a bit closer to heaven. What if you are sprinkled over the most prestigious of mountains that will have everyone talking at the next Kiwanis Club meeting? Like the idea? Then Mount Everest is just for you. What could be more majestic than being dispersed at 29,035 feet on the highest place on Earth? Just find a trekking agency with a reliable Sherpa and you will make cremation history.

If Everest doesn't suit your fancy, here are the highest mountains in the world for each continent:

- *Aconcagua* 6,959m (22,831 ft) S. America: The highest mountain in the Western hemisphere, located in western Argentina, near the Chilean border.

- *Mount McKinley* (Now known as Mount Denali) 6,194m (20,320 ft) N. America: Located in south-central Alaska, in Denali National Park.

- *Mount Kilimanjaro* 5,895m (19,340 ft) Africa: Spanning the peaks of three extinct volcanoes, Kilimanjaro is located in northeastern Tanzania.

- *Mount Elbrus* 5,642m (18,510 ft) Europe: The highest peak of the Caucasus Mountains in southern Russia, it is an extinct volcano with twin cones.

- **Mount Wilhelm** 4,694m (15,400 ft) Oceania: The highest mountain of Papua New Guinea.

- **Vinson Massif** 5,140m (16,864 ft) Antarctica: Situated in the Sentinel Range of the Ellsworth Mountains, home to most of Antarctica's highest mountains.

Did You Know

John Denver, noted singer and songwriter (remember his hit tune "Rocky Mountain High") had his ashes scattered—you guessed it—over the Rocky Mountains. Ansel Adams, the great American landscape photographer has his ashes scattered over Mount Ansel Adams in the Sierra Nevadas. Georgia O'Keeffe had her ashes dropped over the Pedernal Mountain in New Mexico.

---

26. Towering Infernos

You always thought of yourself as intense—a firebrand, a personality burning with a fiery passion. Besides, you have this idea that you want to be warm in the afterlife (but not as Beelzebub's bedroom buddy). What better way to remain pure and warm and extend the perception of your blazing persona than by doing the old heave-ho of your urn right down a blistering, lava-searing volcano?

Some places may not let you get that close, so you may have to find out how close you can get. Moreover, it would really stink if you fell in and had a premature cremation—of yourself. You can find some live volcanoes in Hawaii, Japan, New Zealand, the Caribbean, and Mexico. Here are some of the most famous ones:

- Mount Pelee, St. Pierre, Martinique
- Shishaldin Volcano, Unimak Island, Alaska
- Mount Sakurajima, Kagoshima, Japan
- Popocatepetl, Mexico
- Soufriere Hills, Montserrat, West Indies
- Mt. Bromo, East Java, Indonesia
- Pacaya, Guatemala City, Guatemala
- Kilauea, Hawaii (The Big Island), Hawaii
- Mount Fuji, Japan
- Mount Vesuvius, Italy
- Ruapehu, New Zealand

27. Out with a Bang

If you want a grand and spectacular aerial last goodbye, then consider packing your ashes inside a variety of fireworks and having a grand send-off in a pyrotechnic display that will draw the most delightful "ooohs" and "ahhhhs" ever uttered at a funeral. You can choose from rockets, star shells, and roman candles. You can even go out with a very loud bang with one of those noisy dramatic bursting rockets. And of course, your grand display can be synchronized to your favorite music. Picture this: family and friends staring at the moon and stars. Folks say a few words. Then Beethoven's Fifth or something by Aretha starts to play, and your family looks heavenward. And KA-BOOM, there you go—the fireworks carrying your ashes soaring into the air, then bursting overhead in exquisite patterns and colors, your ethereal dust sparkling in the sky. (25)

Did You Know

Hunter Thompson (the free-wheeling, intoxicant-fueled journalist) and Graham Chapman (of Monty Python fame) were scattered in fireworks displays.

This year's fireworks had a special meaning for George's friends.

28. The Answer, My Friend, Is Blowing in the Wind

How about a way to really cast your fate and ashes to the wind? Then give your dear departed remains a final farewell flight over your favorite spot. If you loved a special beach (like the Big Sur coastline), mountain range (the Rockies), or lake (Winnipesaukee), then you can choose from a number of commercial airplane services that offer aerial dispersion. Although scattering over private land is possible, you might need a landowner's written permission, like being scattered over the original site of Woodstock (Max Yasgur's Farm) or Graceland. (26)

Did You Know

Famed musician Fats Waller had his ashes scattered over Harlem with a flyover by a WWI aviator, Lee Archer, one of the Tuskegee Airmen, who was also known as the "Black Ace."

---

29. Eye of the Storm

Were you a Weather Channel junkie? A storm-watch alert got your adrenaline going, hurricanes gave you goose bumps, and tornadoes made your heart palpitate like a hamster on Ritalin. How about taking your ashes and getting some daring pilot to drop you into the eye of a hurricane or tornado? That twister will swirl your dusty remains so fast that they will get dizzier than a fly in a fertilizer factory. Toto, I have a feeling we're not in Kansas anymore.

30. Around the World in Eighty Days

You may want to take a calmer ride for your eternal ascent. You can, with your ashes placed inside a specially designed giant helium-filled balloon. After the balloon is released, it makes its heavenly climb to about five miles into the atmosphere where the temperature drops to forty degrees below zero. That's when your balloon crystallizes and splits apart, scattering your ashes to the winds. (27)

31. Around the Block in a Couple of Hours

Perhaps you need to watch the costs. That giant balloon thing may not fit your pocketbook. Here's another way to go skyward on the cheap with a bit of randomness and adventure thrown in. Go to your local supermarket or party store, and buy a dozen helium-filled balloons (imagine a dozen smiley faces floating over your town). You can also get balloons special-ordered with the wording you want, like "bon voyage," "happy landings," or "lost soul flying high."

Take a dozen sandwich baggies and fill them with your ashes. Attach each baggie to a separate balloon. Check the weather and wind direction on the day of your service. Pick out a nice launching spot, have the service, and if the wind conditions are right, let the balloons loose. Up, up, and away they go; where they land, nobody knows. Have a little money set aside in case your friends get fined for littering.

32. Beam Me Up, Scotty, and You're Halfway to Heaven

Maybe being blown over the Earth by prevailing winds is still not lofty enough for you. You want to reach higher than that. In fact, you're tired of this planet and leaving it to link up with the cosmos is really what you have in mind. Now you can, courtesy of private aerospace companies. Blast your ashes out of this world by launching your remains along Earth's orbit, onto the lunar surface, or into deep space. You will take off as part of a real space mission and orbit for the length of the satellite's commercial undertaking or as long as the scientific mission lasts. When the satellite reenters earth's atmosphere, you will be one helluva light show. Or if you are sent into deep space, ET may find you, and you'll have a place on his mantelpiece. (28)

Did You Know

What do actor James Doohan (who played Scotty on Star Trek's Enterprise), astronaut Gordon Cooper, Star Trek creator Gene Roddenberry, and LSD pioneer Timothy Leary have in common? They all had their ashes launched into space where few men and women have gone before.

ET speculated if intelligent life was inside the odd container.

VI. At One with the Universe ... and with Others

Okay now. Let's get our heads out of the clouds for a few moments and look at some new and still cosmic dispersal possibilities back here on Earth. We already talked about memorial trees and the possibility of planting a fruit tree with your essentials right under it for nourishment. Remember what we said earlier: If anyone picks a fruit from your tree and eats it, you will become one with them.

Think of the possibilities!

You see, when *they* die, they can also plant a fruit tree with their ashes around the root ball, and other folks will eat their fruit, and then both of you will become one with them. And when these folks buy the farm ... You get the picture, right.

Call it digestive rebirth.

Of course, you should avoid planting fruits with negative connotations that would discourage eating like crab apples, prickly pears, sour grapes, and chokecherries unless that fits your personality.

For the time being, let's look at some other credible edibles to consider beyond the fruit theme with some ideas on how to spread your vitals to a much larger audience.

33. Giving Yourself to Others through Food

If you like the idea of continuing to live on through others after you are gone by means of food, consider tilling your ashes into your vegetable garden or where you grow fruits and berries. Instruct that your ashes should not be dumped into any pumpkin patches in case the kids decide to turn you into next year's jack-o'-lantern instead of a pumpkin pie. Also avoid vegetables that most people don't care for like rutabagas, turnips, and kale. Remember, most people including your friends and family love ordinary vegetables like corn, tomatoes, and French fries.

34. Really Giving Yourself to Others through Food

A friend of mine suggested that if you want to extend yourself to an even larger audience, have your ashes scattered through old Farmer Brown's corn and lettuce fields just before planting season under a full moon. And if that corn is fed to his diary cows, just think of that udder feeling of oneness you will achieve as thousands of kids gulp glasses of milk to wash down their chocolate chip cookies. Better yet, if those cows are beef cows, you might be that tasty new Big Mac people are talking about.

"Wonder if the corn will taste better with Ike's ashes fertilizing the field this year."

35. Quenching Your Thirst for Immortality

I know someone who wanted to have his mother's ashes and her essence (she was said to be a very cool character) absorbed by a *really, really* large number of people. He liked the idea of millions of people soaking her up in a unique way. He suggested that if you like this idea, you should find a reservoir and heave-ho the ashes into the water. In theory, your vital leave-behinds will break up into microscopic particles. People will be gulping you by the glassful, making Starbucks coffee, drinking Scotch with a splash, boiling pasta, and brushing their teeth with you close by. And if it's city water, you can bet you'll taste better than fluoride. Of course, you'd better check with your local health officials for permission (I had to say that for legal reasons, but don't hold what's left of your breath for an okay).

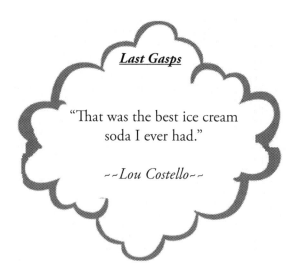

Last Gasps

"That was the best ice cream soda I ever had."

--Lou Costello--

"Strange, this latte seems more full bodied today."

36. A More Direct Approach

Of course, if you have a list of specific people with whom you want to share a bit of you, then make sure you have a celebration after your funeral service where food is served. A sprinkle of your ashes over the onion dip, a spoonful in the lasagna, and a dash in the angel food cake will have people begging for the recipes. Although this is a good source of calcium, check with your state's health officials or family doctor so you don't wind up like Sweeney Todd.

Here lie the bones
of Joseph Jones
Who ate while he was able.
But once overfed,
he dropt down dead
And fell beneath the table.
When from the tomb,
to meet his doom,
He arises amidst sinners.
Since he must dwell
in heaven or hell,
Take him-whichever
gives the best dinners.

VIII. Mostly Amusing Options

We are taught to think that funerals and last rites need to have dignity. Says who? Why not consider some undignified ideas if you have a penchant for last laughs, irony, and humor? All the things that you never said and wished you had can at last be articulated in your final statement to the world or a few choice people. Do you really care at this point what anybody will think? Maybe, depending on what you choose, they will actually think better of you.

37. Revenge Tastes So Sweet

Maybe you couldn't care less about your ashes and don't want to spend a lot of time fussing over poetic ways to scatter yourself into eternity. But you have a few people on your "I will never send them a holiday card" list that for one reason or another didn't treat you with the respect you deserved. So why not surprise them with the chore of figuring out what to do with your ashes as your way of getting even? Send them your ashes through the US postal service in a simple, easy-on-your-pocketbook container with an appropriate note. (29)

Here are some candidates for your karmic payback:

- Your ex-wife who got all the money
- Your ex-husband who was always a lazy schmuck and diddled his secretary thinking you were too thick to notice
- That boss who never once said "good job" or gave you a decent raise
- The car mechanic who told you that you needed repairs you never needed
- The surgeon who told you that you had to have an unnecessary operation so he could pay for his new kidney-shaped swimming pool
- That girl or guy in high school you had a crush on who never gave you the time of day

- Any relative, in-law, sibling, or family member who never gave you a break and thought that making wisecracks about you and why you were born was hilarious
- That neighbor who called the police whenever you played the Stones too loud or borrowed tools and never returned them
- Your building's superintendent who never fixed the dripping faucets, the broken windows, and the toilet that never flushed right
- That hard-assed teacher who flunked you because your term paper wasn't double-spaced (assuming she is still alive)
- That ex-friend who never paid back the money you lent him
- All the literary agents who said your book was not for them
- The publisher who would publish a book like this instead of your great work of literature

Quotable Quotes

"The best revenge is living long enough to be a problem to your children."

--Unknown--

38. You Party Animal

Revenge has its place, and so does a bit of fun. So how about making your send-off a bit more playful for the folks coming to your funeral service? Hold it outdoors at your favorite picnic spot, apple orchard, or public park, or anyplace that enables you to hang something from above (a rafter will do for an inside setting). Pay the minister, rabbi, imam, or priest a few extra bucks to come dressed like a clown, say a few chosen words, and then switch on a boom box that blasts something from the Village People sung in Swedish.

The cleric points and the mourners turn to see that hanging from a tree limb is a huge piñata of a giant head, the very spitting image of you. (30) The piñata is filled with all sorts of goodies including your ashes, which are now nestled in a dozen plastic eggs. Everyone gets a chance to whack you. More important, you won't get a headache once all the whacking is done, but you will probably give your guests a few big ones. It all depends on what goodies you select.

Here are some ideas:

- Your last will and testament, that everyone thought was lost, written in Aramaic
- Your entire inheritance in the form of gold coins (he or she who scrambles the fastest inherits the mostest)
- Sets of keys that fit in a dozen cars in the parking lot (you big spender, you)
- Sets of keys that fit into nothing in the parking lot
- Happy Meal gift certificates (since you left most of your money to the Feline Rescue League)
- Ten sessions of family therapy to help process all the damage you did as a parent (since you spent their inheritance already and only left them Happy Meals)

Little did Grandpa's relatives know that Grandpa's piñata was filled with Grandpa.

39. Life Is a Roller Coaster

Remember all those fun times at Coney Island, or the state fair, or any other amusement park you went to as a kid? How about having your final send-off from a roller coaster (release from the back seat for consideration of blow-back on other riders)? You can also spin into the atmospheric atmosphere from a merry-go-round, Tilt-A-Whirl, Roundup, or Ferris wheel. Make sure to have someone check the wind direction so your ashes don't drift too close to the cotton candy stand.

40. Clowning Around

You always loved the circus. The acrobats, the clowns, the elephant dung. Make this a family affair, and get tickets to the circus when it comes to town. Have them get there early, since most circuses let you mingle with the performers before the big show begins. Have your party of family and friends go to center ring and sprinkle you discreetly around. Maybe sneak a little bit of you in the cannon before they do the human cannonball act. Now that's a grand finale!

Last Gasps

"How were the receipts today in Madison Square Garden?"

~~*P.T. Barnum*~~

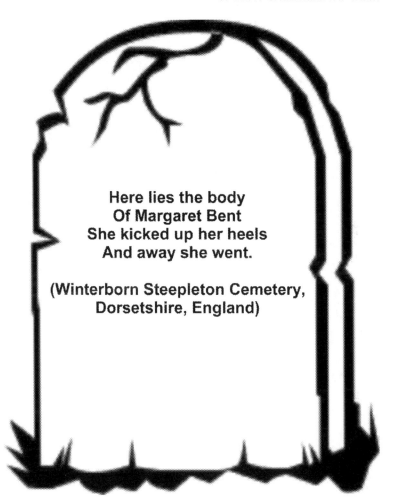

Here lies the body
Of Margaret Bent
She kicked up her heels
And away she went.

(Winterborn Steepleton Cemetery,
Dorsetshire, England)

IX. Disposable Options

These few options are for those who really don't care much about how their ashes are disposed and want to make that clear with a bit of black humor.

41. Too-Da-Loo and Down the Loo

This idea assumes you really don't care what happens to your ashes. If that's the case, then the most obvious way of disposal is—you guessed it—down the toilet. Nothing subtle about this method. You can remind everyone gathered in the bathroom for the service that even *you* thought you were a knucklehead to the very end. Sadly, they might agree. The good news is that you will be purified at last although this spiritual cleansing process that will take place at your city's sewage treatment plant. If you have a septic system instead, purification will stay local, and your buddies can pay their last respects around your leaching field.

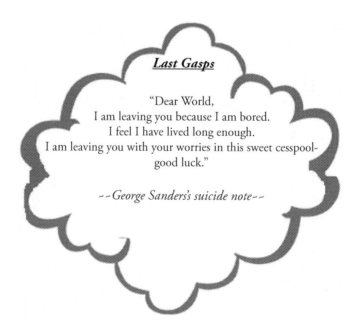

Last Gasps

"Dear World,
I am leaving you because I am bored.
I feel I have lived long enough.
I am leaving you with your worries in this sweet cesspool-
good luck."

--George Sanders's suicide note--

Fred's friends hoped one good flush would do.

42. Sink or Swim

Along the lines of ashes flushed down the porcelain throne, you might consider dumping your ashes down the sink à la the garbage disposal. You'll end up in the same place, just taking a different route. On the bright side, having your mourners in the kitchen for the service may be better than the bathroom since you can serve appetizers and your very favorite cocktails. Pass the onion dip, will ya?

43. Trash Night

Wait till the garbage man shows up early Tuesday morning to see a group of your pals gathered around a trash can, weeping away and singing your praises. Somewhere in between the coffee grinds, egg shells, and pizza crusts are your ashes neatly bundled in a biodegradable paper bag from Trader Joe's. Off to the dump you go, into the giant compost heap in the sky.

44. Fluffy Would Be Happy

Maybe you want to offer some redeeming last statement of usefulness. How about taking those ashes and mixing them into

Fluffy's kitty litter. Fluffy, the only real warm-blooded friend you ever had, will certainly appreciate this, since you never bought him the clumping kind he always wanted.

"Granny said to mix her ashes in with your kitty litter, and that's that!"

45. A Life Aquatic

Fish have feelings too. If it's good enough for Fluffy, then let's not forget your other favorite pet that just happens to be cold-blooded and has no eyelids. Yes, Goldie the Goldfish and you had a very special relationship not many people could understand. She didn't mind you staring at her for hours, that annoying tapping on the glass to get her attention, or forgetting to clean the filter so that the water turned a yucky yellow.

One way you can still remain close to her is by having yourself made into good-quality gravel to be layered at the bottom of her aquarium. Besides, being transformed into gravel will give you a useful purpose in life—which, let's face it, was elusive—as you assist in the biological filtration to support a healthy habitat in Goldie's tank. If you want to go out in style, consider having yourself made into aquarium gravel in a variety of stunning colors, since Goldie the Goldfish always thought you were a fairly dull dresser.

He got a fish-bone
caught in his throat
And then he sang
an angel note.

46. On the Road Again

If you didn't own a cat or a fish but like the idea of usefulness, then have your ashes dumped at the city highway department's rock-salt pile to be spread on the icy roads when winter's snows begin. You might actually help save a life. Finally people will have to admit that you were the salt of the earth and actually had great redemptive qualities.

47. Recycle Your Soul

Another way for karmic redemption is to put yourself back into the material life you just left. Pour your ashes into the glass bottles and plastic containers that you would normally recycle.

The next time someone swigs a Coke, it may give people an out-of-body lift. Or have your executors layer your ashes in between the newspapers and the trashy fiction you used to read. These can be recycled into pulp that will make its way into a variety of reading materials. That way you can really have the last word.

48. Anger Management Once You're Gone

If you reach any level of self-awareness before you exit stage left, maybe you will have finally realized that you weren't the saint you thought you were. Since you probably didn't work out your resentments and anger over all those people who tried to love you while you were still occupying space and taking in air, how about giving the people you left behind a way to vent? Buy them a punching bag with your ashes packed inside. They can slam away and will feel much better, and you won't feel a thing. (31)

Quotable Quotes

"Happiness is having a large, loving, caring, close-knit family in another city.

~~George Burns~~

X. Scattering Places

We've talked a lot about **how** you may want to be scattered. Let's get back to some more ideas about **where** you can get strewn, sprinkled, or spread. The number of places you can be scattered over, around, above, and below on our planet is infinite. Locations that you might be drawn to can be tied to your love of the outdoors, places that have to do with your personal history, things you liked to do, unusual interests that perked up your life, or ideas that appealed to your quirky and unique sense of humor that no one ever got.

There are oodles of ideas from which you can choose, before you take that eternal snooze. And remember, you aren't limited to one spot. You can drive those you leave behind crazy by insisting that you be scattered in a bunch of places. Call it payback for all the times they drove you crazy with their unreasonable demands.

Did You Know

Howard Keel, famed actor-singer in some of the most popular musicals of the 1950s, such as Annie Get Your Gun, Showboat, and Kiss Me Kate was scattered around his favorite places including the Mere Golf Club, Liverpool's John Lennon Airport, and various settings in Tuscany, Italy.

---

49. A Snow-White Send-Off

This would certainly get Walt hot under the collar if he alive today, so I won't recommend it, but my second cousin once removed professed a love of Mickey and friends. When she goes to that magic kingdom in the sky, she wants to be scattered throughout Disneyland (or Disney World if she happens to expire in Orlando).

Your ashes—and you by association—can undyingly experience the enchantment of any or all of Disney's fanciful theme parks. Whether you choose Disneyland in Anaheim, California, or Disney World in Orlando, Florida, your divine essence can linger over the Magic Kingdom, Frontierland, Epcot Center, or Space Mountain. Let your spirit inspire everyone in your family, group of friends, and even the Japanese tourists you never got to meet—all those who flock like lemmings to make the obligatory pilgrimage to the epicenter of our G-rated American kitschy culture. *It's a Small World*, indeed. (32)

The tourists thought that there was something very otherworldly about Tink's magic dust.

50. Life's a Gamble

If you want an epicenter of American culture but of a different sort, let's talk Vegas. You were full of craps, were never flush, and liked to watch revolving balls.

We're not talking about your personality; we're talking about your love of gambling. You treasured poker, craps, roulette, and the slots; and when nothing else was available you did bingo at

Saint Mary's with the blue-haired ladies. What better place to roll your last dice than in Las Vegas?

Your ashes can be showered down the Strip or dealt around the grounds of the Golden Nugget, Bellagio's, or the MGM Grand. Or how about sprinkling a bit of you around the slot machine that stole your money night after night? Or imagine a dash of you given to an Elvis impersonator or delivered as an anonymous gift to the couple going into that drive-thru wedding chapel. Spread yourself around town just like the money you blew, and it will be the best bet you ever made. (33)

Did You Know

Palm Mortuary in Las Vegas now offers funeral backdrops with giant playing cards, enormous casino chips, oversized dice, and a towering slot machine to memorialize the dear departed to give gamblers that special send-off.

Emma finally got Fred to play bingo with her best friend Martha.

51. School Daze

Did you ever feel like you weren't the brightest light on the Christmas tree or menorah? Your academic career may have been middling at best. You were easily distracted by the hedonistic rites of passage at college, making shallow friends, and figuring out what your purpose in life was, other than to be supported by your parents forever.

Or maybe you actually were the sharpest knife in the drawer, had perfect SAT scores, and were accepted to one of those colleges with ivy growing over its hallowed walls. A genius or not, college just might have been the best years of your life where you could indulge your intellectual pursuits, take mind-altering classes, drink like a fish, and finally acquire a significant other.

If those times still bring a smile to your face, why not scatter your ashes around your alma mater's campus? Or if you didn't get into one of those snooty Ivy League schools, place your remains at the school you would have liked to attend. Just think … no tuition, no exams, and no studying—what could be better?

Did You Know

Charles Starrett, known for his cowboy roles (the Durango Kid) and in films like The Mask of Fu Manchu (with Boris Karloff), was scattered by air over his alma mater, Dartmouth College.

Langston Hughes, the famous poet, had his ashes buried under the floorboards of the Schomburg Library of African American Culture in Harlem, under a plaque inscribed with one of his poems.

---

52. Church Scatterings

You may want to get a few extra points in before you meet up with Saint Peter. Never much of a churchgoer, you might want to increase your odds for getting through the pearly gates by scattering your ashes on the grounds of a venerable church. Here is a list of notable churches you can consider:

- Saint Peter's Basilica in the Vatican (Rome)
- Saint Patrick's Cathedral (New York City)
- Saint Paul's Cathedral (London)
- Notre Dame (Paris)
- The Duomo (Cathedral of Florence)
- Church of the Holy Sepulcher (Jerusalem)
- Abyssinian Baptist Church (Harlem, NY)
- Hagia Sophia (Istanbul)
- Saint Basil the Blessed (Moscow)
- Saint Stephen's (Vienna)

<hr>

Quotable Quotes

"Churches welcome all denominations, but most prefer fives and tens."

~~Anonymous~~

<hr>

53. The Chosen People Can't Do This

As in Islam, Orthodox Jews are not supposed to be cremated. If you are Jewish, *do not* scatter yourself at these sites, which are considered most holy to the Chosen People:

- The Wailing Wall (Jerusalem)
- Tomb of Moses, under Siyagha church, Mount Nebo, Jordan
- The Stage or Carnegie Delicatessens (New York City)
- Anywhere in south Florida
- On the old grounds of Grossinger's Hotel in the Catskills
- Loehmanns or Filenes' basement during a sale
- Opening Night at *Fiddler on the Roof*

- Zabar's (New York City)
- The town of Kayseri in central Turkey where pastrami was invented
- The Bromo Seltzer tower (Baltimore) since heartburn was invented by the Jews (with some *agita* help from Italians)
- Sheboygan, Wisconsin (where Jackie Mason was born)

54. Historic Scatterings

Perhaps you were a history buff. What better way to celebrate your hobby than being scattered on your much-loved historic site? Think of your ashes mulched into the soil of your favorite president's birthplace or scattered around Plymouth Rock, over the sandy runway next to Kitty Hawk, or around Davy Crockett's last stand at the Alamo.

55. Military Scatterings

If you liked the idea of the Alamo and being scattered over a battlefield, think of all the other battlefields you can consider—Gettysburg, Bunker Hill, or Wounded Knee, to name a few. Or if you want something overseas, how about Normandy, Hastings (as in the Battle of Hastings, 1066), or Troy (as in Helen of).

The Department of Veterans Affairs' (VA) National Cemetery Administration maintains 125 national cemeteries in 39 states (and Puerto Rico) as well as 33 soldier's lots and monument sites. Hup-two-three-four, get those ashes out the door.

Did You Know

Arlington National Cemetery has one of the larger columbariums for cremains in the country. Currently, there are over 38,500 niches. When construction is complete, there will be a total of over 60,000 niches; capacity for more than 100,000 cremains. Any honorably discharged veteran is eligible for inurnment in the columbarium. *

* arlingtoncemetery.org

---

56. Feel the Pain

This world has had its share of grief and sorrow brought on by the people who inhabit it. Your heart has always been heavy with pervasive inhumanity to man and woman. Instead of denying our history of heartlessness, you want to make a statement to those you leave behind—a reminder that we must never forget what we have done to each other and what we should not repeat. You could have your ashes scattered at one of those terrible places in history so, when your grandchildren ask where you are buried, they will learn that you are with the souls at Auschwitz or the killing fields of Cambodia, at Pearl Harbor or Dresden, along the Bear River near Preston, Idaho (where the Shoshone Indian massacre at Boa Ogoi took place), Rwanda, Darfur, or the World Trade Center. Unfortunately, there are too many more to list.

Did You Know

Crew members who were assigned to the USS Arizona on December 7, 1941 (Pearl Harbor Day), have the right to have their cremains interred inside the barbette of gun turret four by National Park Service divers. In addition, any Pearl Harbor survivor can have their ashes scattered over the place in the harbor where their ship was located during the attack.

---

57. I Love Paris in the Springtime

Before you get too bummed out by number 56, let's get your mind to travel to a more pleasant place. Maybe you once took the perfect trip to Europe. You have great memories of those famous places that every tourist had to visit, snapping away with your camera like Ansel Adams on double espresso. If you didn't, there's no reason why you still can't. Either way, you can pick the one tourist place closest to your heart to be scattered—or be an afterlife tourist and get dropped off at as many sites as you wish. Here's a list of cool places to be relocated in your next life as the never-ending sightseer:

- Swept away from the top of the Eiffel Tower
- Sprinkled along Venice's Grand Canal
- Strewn around Big Ben
- Tossed on the rails of the Paris Metro
- Left off at the Arc de Triomphe
- Spread through Amsterdam's Red Light District
- Artfully placed outside the Louvre
- Dropped inside the Parthenon in Athens
- Released within the Coliseum in Rome
- Scattered about Buckingham Palace
- Placed on the grounds of Westminster Abbey
- Thrown over the bulwarks of Heidelberg Castle
- Lobbed from the James Joyce Tower in Dublin
- Pitched from the top of Gaudí's Sagrada Familia in Barcelona
- Left at what remains of the Berlin Wall
- Blended in with the other ashes at Pompeii

You might want to pick up a book entitled *1000 Places to Visit before You Die*, by Patricia Schultz, for more ideas.

All of Paris wondered what that funny haze was that floated away from the Eiffel tower.

58. America, the Beautiful

Then again, how about the good old US of A for scattering? Why not select a beautiful scenic spot in one of the national parks listed below? Of course, check for any permission requirements before scattering. (34)

- Acadia (Maine)
- Apostle Islands (Wisconsin)
- Bryce Canyon (Utah)
- ape Cod (Massachusetts)
- Death Valley & Mojave (California)
- Everglades (Florida)
- Glacier (Montana)
- Grand Canyon (Arizona)
- Grand Teton (Wyoming)
- Great Smoky Mountains (Tennessee)
- Rocky Mountain (Colorado)
- White Mountains (New Hampshire)
- Yellowstone (Wyoming)
- Yosemite (California)
- Zion (Utah)

59. Born in the USA

If you'd prefer a patriotic scattering, then check these spots out for dispersal:

- Statue of Liberty (New York City)
- Washington Monument (Washington DC)
- Valley Forge (Valley Forge National Park, Pennsylvania)
- Liberty Bell (Philadelphia, Pennsylvania)
- Arlington House – The Robert E. Lee Memorial (McLean, Virginia)
- Arlington National Cemetery (Arlington, Virginia)
- Lincoln Memorial (Washington DC)
- Monticello (Thomas Jefferson's home—Virginia Piedmont, Virginia)

- Antietam National Battlefield (Sharpsburg, Maryland)
- Mount Rushmore (South Dakota)
- Plymouth Rock (Massachusetts)
- Old Ironsides (Boston Harbor)
- Bunker Hill (Boston)

60. Other Very Cool Places

Here is a mishmash of cool places to get scattered if nothing has struck a chord so far:

Atop the Empire State Building
You'd be in good company with King Kong, Fay Wray, and the 34 people who have jumped to their deaths.

Into the Panama Canal
Approximately fifty-one miles long, with twelve thousand ships gliding through each year, the nine-hour trip gives you plenty of time to get sprinkled from the Caribbean to the Pacific.

Over a bridge (here are a few suggestions, and probably some sites you never even knew about):

- Dunlaps Creek Bridge, oldest iron bridge in America (Brownsville, Pennsylvania)
- Brooklyn Bridge, oldest surviving suspension bridge in America (Brooklyn, NY)
- Smithfield Street Bridge, oldest through-truss bridge (Pittsburgh, Pennsylvania)
- Kinzua Viaduct, one of the oldest surviving viaduct bridges (former Erie Railroad in Pennsylvania)
- The Arthur Ravenel Jr. Bridge, longest cable-stayed bridge (Charleston, South Carolina)
- The Bath-Haverhill Covered Bridge, oldest still-functioning covered bridge in America (Bath, New Hampshire)

Anywhere in Key West, Florida

For an eclectic site, imagine a place that appealed to such varied personalities as Harry Truman, Ernest Hemingway, Tennessee Williams, and swashbuckling pirates. And of course if you are gay, then your ashes can whoop it up since it's the vacation mecca for gay and lesbian tourists. Better yet, it's the only "frost-free" city in the continental US and just ninety miles away from a real Cuban cigar.

Last Gasps

"Either the wallpaper goes, or I do."

~~Oscar Wilde~~

Under the sands of Ipanema Beach, Rio de Janeiro, Brazil

Here's a vicarious option in an exotic locale where the bronzed boys play soccer on the sand in their scanty Speedos and the girls sunbathe in their famously skimpy dental-floss bikinis. Those hotty guys and gals in thongs will have your ashes tickle their toes and bottoms and might just bring you back to life.

On Easter Island

For a headstone no one can top, have your ashes dug into a hole next to one of Easter Island's famous giant stone monoliths, known as moai, which mark the coastline. Once a thriving culture with an advanced social order, Easter Island declined into bloody civil war and, evidently, cannibalism. The statues have been attributed to alien visitors, occupants of a lost continent, and the Rapa Nui. Once you're there, you won't really care.

Around the Great Pyramid, Giza, Egypt ... Or How about the Sphinx

You may want to think twice about being strewn around the Great Pyramid of the Egyptian pharaoh Khufu (died 2566 BC), who is believed by some to have been a ruthless and cruel despot. You might choose instead the Sphinx with the body of a lion and the head of a king or god, which has come to symbolize strength and wisdom. Your choice.

"Exactly which of the Great Pyramids did Frank want to be strewn?"

At the Taj Mahal, India

In 1648, the Taj Mahal (meaning Crown Palace) was built by Mughal Emperor Shah Jahan in the memory of his wife and queen Mumtaz Mahal at Agra, India. It took twenty-two years to construct, using 20,000 workers. You might consider being dropped off at the reflecting pool that approaches the main gate of this mausoleum.

During a Kenyan animal safari
Not *Out of Africa* but *Back to Africa*, whence humans came. Have your buddies hot-air balloon over the Masai Mara plains with a few spoonfuls of your ashes dropped from above. Then land at one of villages of the Samburu or Masai tribes along the way and see if they will honor you with a blood and milk Great Ox feast ceremony. For a final deposit, pay a visit to Jane Goodall's Tchimpounga Sanctuary. No one is going to make a monkey out of you anymore.

La Brea Tar Pits, Los Ángeles
It's a sticky ending, but you'll be in good company with all the other antediluvians that humped around southern California from 8,000 to 40,000 years ago. Most important, you will have thousands of visitors to this now-famous tourist spot containing one of the richest, best preserved, and best studied collections of Pleistocene vertebrates. Here's a chance for your prehistoric ideas to be finally be appreciated.

Great Wall of China
You better go easy on the dusting if you want to cover the entire length of the Great Wall, which is the longest fortified line ever constructed and can be seen from the moon. It zigzags 1,500 miles, was built entirely by hand, and took hundreds of years to complete. Instead of a spoon to ladle you out, try chopsticks.

The Barringer Meteorite Crater (a.k.a. "Meteor Crater")
Weighing roughly 300,000 tons, the Barringer meteorite was traveling at a speed of 28,600 miles per hour when it hit the earth at 150 times the force of the atomic bomb that destroyed Hiroshima. Scientists believe that the crater was created approximately 50,000 years ago by a meteorite, which may have

originated in the interior of a small planet. It left a gigantic hole in the middle of the Arizona desert that is nearly a mile wide and 570 feet deep. That's the deepest grave you'll ever find. If they always said you were a space shot, what better place to be tossed.

Machu Picchu, Peru

You may not have been treated like a king or queen in your own home, but you can at least be laid to rest like one. Built by Pachacuti Inca Yupanqui, an Incan ruler, between AD 1460 and 1470, Machu Picchu was most likely a royal estate and religious retreat, with about twelve hundred people living in and around it, most of them women, children, and priests.

Stonehenge

This ancient monument of huge, rough-cut stones standing alone on the Salisbury Plain in Wiltshire, England, has captured imaginations for centuries. No one knows exactly who placed them there or why. Speculation ranges from human sacrifice to astronomy. It seems to have been designed to allow observation of astronomical phenomena—summer and winter solstices, eclipses, and more. Or maybe it was designed just for you and your ashes.

Sites associated with assassinations

If you are feeling like a victim with the world against you, consider these sad places and the people who came to abrupt and violent ends: Presidents Lincoln (Ford Theatre, DC), Garfield, and McKinley; Malcolm X (Audubon Ballroom, NYC), Martin Luther King Jr. (Memphis), John (Dealey Plaza–the Grassy Knoll, Dallas) and Bobby Kennedy (Ambassador Hotel, LA; torn down in 2006 for a school), Anwar Sadat (Cairo), and John Lennon (the Dakota apartment building, NYC).

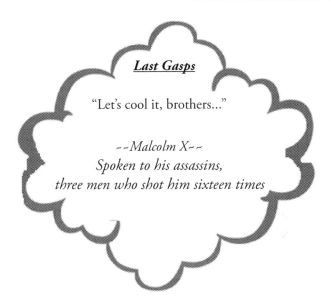

Last Gasps

"Let's cool it, brothers..."

--Malcolm X--
Spoken to his assassins,
three men who shot him sixteen times

Death Valley

What could be more fitting than to be blown over a desert named Death Valley. Oh, the mockery of it! Death Valley is one of the hottest places on this planet with summer temperatures reaching well over a hundred degrees Fahrenheit, with an average rainfall of only 1.96 inches a year, making it the driest in the United States. Mold and mildew will never be a problem for you again since your ashes will always remain drier than a mouthful of mummy wrappings.

Did You Know

Wally Cox had his ashes mingled with those of Marlon Brando and another friend and scattered in Death Valley, California. Brando had his ashes scattered partly in Tahiti and partly in Death Valley.

XI. Arts, Crafts, and Some Other Precious Ideas

We have discussed being scattered into places. What about being *placed into things* or *made into things*? That creative streak in you can never die, or so you hope. Why not prove that it won't by having your ashes transformed into things of beauty, both practical and otherwise?

61. A Diamond Lasts Forever, and So Will You

Did the people you love think of you as frugal? Do you want to ensure that your remains are not gathering dust on a bookshelf or mantelpiece? How about turning yourself into something of so much value that you can become a treasured heirloom in your family, handed down with awe for generations to come.

Now you can.

Companies can fashion a one-of-a-kind real diamond from the carbon residue contained in your ashes—a treasured memorial to your exceptional life. How about a pair of earrings for your widow, the ones she wanted for your anniversary but got a membership to Weight Watchers instead? Or maybe a diamond pinky ring for your husband who always wanted to look like a Mafia boss. Or consider a diamond pendant for your daughter to make up for all those months you grounded her—or better yet, a tiara so she can be instated as the true princess you dearly loved. Of course, we're talking some real bucks here, ranging from about $4,000 to $20,000 depending on how big a carat you want to be turned into. Come on, big spender! You can't take it with you. (35)

Little did King Henry know that his favorite diamond was really Uncle Charles.

62. And Then There's Costume Jewelry

Maybe diamonds just aren't your style, you being more of a zircon kind of person anyway. Don't sweat it, because there is a low-cost option for the jewelry idea. How about putting a small portion of your ashes in an assortment of heart-shaped pendants, cremation cylinders, or rosary beads? Pendants are available in 14k gold or sterling silver and include a funnel, glue, and instructions to fill and seal the pendant. These lovely accessories containing your remains can be worn around the necks of loved ones. Wouldn't these make a great last gift from you for the holidays? (36)

63. You Were Always a Masterpiece

Here's another idea if you consider yourself an art lover. Why not be transformed into a work of art that would make Mona Lisa smile. That's right; a painted masterpiece with your ashes mixed into the pigments, giving you thousands of pictorial possibilities to explore.

"Mom always said she would look good as the Mona Lisa."

Here's what to do. Find a painter you respect with skill and versatility. Then decide what the subject of the painting will be. The obvious is a self-portrait, but how about having your ash-loaded colors finding themselves in a reproduction of Leonardo da Vinci's *Last Supper*, Andy Warhol's *Campbell's Soup Can*, or some surrealistic melted-clock landscape by Dalí? Another thought is choosing a really famous still-living artist and being mixed into his or her oils or acrylics. With any luck, you could wind up in an exhibition at the Museum of Modern Art. Just hope that the art critics don't pan the show.

Did You Know

Wayne Gilbert, Houston, Texas, gallery owner and artist, has attracted local and national attention for his ongoing series of paintings using cremains. Gilbert used to mix the cremains with paint, but stopped once he noticed that each person's ashes had their own subtle earth-tone color. To preserve the natural color, Gilbert now mixes the cremains with a clear gel, turning them into individualistic "paint."

---

* .blogs.chron.com/artbeat

64. Urban Art and Tag You're It

Maybe you like the idea of paint and art ... but not as a painting hung on a wall. You want something that makes a statement that the general population can appreciate. Something that is more accessible than a hoity-toity museum where people have to fork over twenty bucks for the admission fee just to pay homage to you.

The answer is "tagging," that ever-present graffiti you see scrawled on every city wall, bus, and underpass in the world. You can find a wealth of graffiti artists on the Web. All you need to do is create your distinct tag, maybe some hip-hop letters, a fantasy image with unicorns, or Castro French-kissing our former vice president. Pick the spots you want tagged, and then you will be installed as a vaunted urban legend, at least till they power-wash you off the wall. In death, you will become the art *gangsta* you always wanted to be by supporting street art and reclaiming public space. Write on, brothers and sisters! (37)

65. Lasting in Latex

Okay, forget these high-brow suggestions of masterpiece paintings and politically charged graffiti proclamations. Have your pals go to Home Depot and buy a few gallons of outdoor exterior latex or oil-based paint (I prefer oil-based myself) and mix you up. Doesn't your house need painting? Or how about donating the paint to a Habitat for Humanity project? Whichever you choose, you will get eternal, external soul-redeeming coverage. You can also consider painting other things with your everlasting pigments:

- Kitchen chairs (but you will need to put up with flatulent guests)
- Park benches (make sure you are comfortable with bums and winos sleeping on top of you)
- Fences (do good neighbors make)

> ▪ Baby cribs (lead-free paint, please, as you watch over your grandkids' souls)

66. Let Your Grandkids Commemorate You

Wonder what your grandchildren thought of you? Let them express all those nice memories in art with a bit of you inside. They can make crayons with a dash of your karmic leftovers. What they will need: (38)

- ▪ Old and broken crayons
- ▪ Mold (you can use any shape you like)
- ▪ Crock-Pot
- ▪ Spoon to ladle melted crayon wax
- ▪ A bit of your ashes nicely pulverized
- ▪ Acid-free drawing paper

Have an adult supervise. Get rid of the wrappers from the old crayon stubs and sort them by color. Put the stubs—one color at a time—into a Crock-Pot, and set the temperature at "high." Stir in your ashes, and cook it for bit until melted, then reset heat to "low." Spoon liquid into crayon molds. Let them cool and harden and—voilà—you have new all-about-you crayons. Hand out the acid-free paper, which will last for decades, and have the kids start drawing. This will be one time in your life when you want to be framed.

Quotable Quotes

"Art, like morality, consists of drawing the line somewhere."

~~G. K. Chesterton~~

---

67. 'Tis the Season to Be Jolly

What better way to be remembered—well, at least once a year—than by pouring your ashes into one of those lovely Christmas bulbs? Just remove the clips from the top of the bulb, and get poured inside the bulb through a small hand funnel. You can have your executors custom-decorate the bulbs with pictures of you or pithy sayings like "hanging tough." If you are Jewish, have your ashes placed into drilled holes inside a menorah. You can continue to light up the family's life for at least eight days (or nights) a year.

68. You Had a Magnetic Personality

If you want people to see more of you than they did when you were alive, then get displayed on a spot that people go to at least ten times a day. No, it's not on the mantelpiece or a bookshelf. It's the refrigerator! And what better way to remind them of your time on earth than being made into a refrigerator magnet? All you need are strong magnets and some imagination, and a make-a-magnet kit, which can purchased at many arts and crafts stores.

Add some powdered pigment to make the magnets more cheerful. Or create a little portrait of yourself using paint mixed with your ashes. And if you want to be really generous, buy everyone a refrigerator to attach the magnet. (39)

Quotable Quotes

"One reason people get divorced is that they run out of gift ideas."

--Robert Byrne--

---

69. They'll Be Dyeing for You

Here's an idea that will wear on people, but in a good way. You can make a unique fashion statement by designing apparel using dyes that have you mixed in with them. You can get dyes with colors that are brilliant and permanent and won't fade, even after repeated washings.

If you have fond memories of those Age of Aquarius music festivals you used to grace with your presence, how about bequeathing tie-dyed T-shirts to everyone who attends your memorial service? If not clothes, then how about a prayer flag like the ones the Tibetans make? Prayer flags are decorated with lucky symbols, invocations, and mantras. For centuries Buddhists have placed these flags outside their homes so that the wind can carry the good vibrations across the countryside and beyond. Prayer flags bring happiness, longevity, and riches to the flag planter and those around them. What better gift from someone on their way to a cosmic voyage? (40)

70. Ashes to Ashes

Another crafty idea is to mix your ashes into ceramic clay that can be made into pottery. Have a potter make vases, mugs, bowls, or any other ceramic piece of your choosing. They can be handed out at your service or when your will is read. For a bit of irony, have the potter make an assortment of *ash*trays as mementos. Your friends and family are sure to have a *glazed* look followed by a smile.

"I hope Grandma's ashes won't mess up my glaze."

71. For Whom the Bell Tolls

If you are a churchgoer, then this idea may appeal to you. Find a bell-maker who can hand-cast a bell from a mold you select, adding your ashes into the bronze. Donate the bell to your church. What a joyous sound you will make. Better yet, you will never get an earache. (41)

72. Praise the Lord

If you are Christian, you might consider having a crucifix made using a cast with your ashes added into the casting. Depending on your sense of humor or propriety, donate it to your church where it might be placed above the altar. What greater way not to miss any more sermons?

Here lies an Atheist
All dressed up
And no place to go...

XII. Make Something of Yourself Already

We have been talking about making things that are of a certain size and reasonable scale. How about thinking really large now? There are many ways to instill your spirit in grander things and places that will remain earthbound after your essence heads to more blissful pastures. Let's take a look at a few structurally sound suggestions.

73. The Donald

Perhaps you were a big fan of *The Apprentice* and Donald Trump. You wished you could have been as successful as Mr. Trump and part of his building empire or anyone else's. Well now you can. Research what new building projects are being developed. Pick the one that fascinates you the most. Have your executors take your ashes to the building site you've selected and find the nearest cement truck. Give the driver a hundred bucks to toss your ashes into the mix. When the foundation is poured, you will be the spiritual foundation on which the next casino, hotel, or luxury condo complex will rest. Better yet, you will have resolved that edifice complex you never worked through.

74. Not the Donald

Then again, maybe you were never a big fan of the Donald, and especially befuddled by that hairdo you couldn't figure out. But the idea of being part of a glorious man-made structure, like a new bridge or skyscraper, makes your loins feel as hard as a flying buttress. Once again, research what new buildings or public projects are in the works. Pick one that catches your fancy. Have your executors take your ashes to the company that will supply the contractor with the steel girders. Give the guy at the smelter a hundred bucks to toss your ashes into the molten mix. When the steel superstructure is erected, you will have the most riveting experience of your afterlife.

Last Gasps

"Last words are for fools who haven't said enough."

~~Karl Marx~~

Quotable Quotes

"A government which robs Peter to pay Paul can always depend on the support of Paul."

~~George Bernard Shaw~~
(1856–1950)

---

75. Firming Up Some Other Constructive Ideas

Of course, there are many other options for you if you like being part of society's infrastructure. Add your ashes to cement for:

- Sidewalks (recommended if you are a podiatrist: think of all those feet you can touch)
- Highways (think of those tires running over you as a tireless massage)

- Sewer pipes (you must have a strong self-image before selecting this one)
- Culverts (this time the sound of running water won't remind you of the bladder problems you might have had)
- Retaining walls (if you're the type who always bore up)
- Basement floors (if you want to be really grounded)
- Benches (take a load off those still trucking around)
- Swimming pools (you didn't like the burial at sea thing, and wanted to stay local; but remember what kids do in pools)
- Driveways (if it's your own, you can stay close to home)
- Patios (you can still be part of those family barbeques and drinks at sunset)
- Cement burial vaults (ah, think of the irony)

"Harry had a bit of edifice complex so I poured him into the cement."

XIII. Crunchy Granola Ideas

You can finally come out of the closet, oh tie-dyed one. You always wished you'd been at Woodstock—or maybe you were and now, as a card-carrying Republican, could never admit it to your corporate cronies. You used to dream about taking yoga classes, chanting with Ram Dass, hugging men and women without feeling homophobic, and listening to Janis Ian. Now you can walk on the wild side—do something really alternative—a touchy-feely, gone-with-the-wind type of thing.

76. Make a Political Statement

Did you feel that your vote never really counted? It kills you that this knucklehead is now—or was—your mayor, congressional rep, senator, president, dogcatcher, whatever elected official. Big-city politics, small-town politics—it's all politics. Well, it's not too late to have the last laugh. Here are a few ideas:

- You might consider a midnight ash-scattering over or around the selected elected official's lawn. Good chance the vaunted bureaucrat or whomever you chose will get their Oxfords a bit dusty when they give their next disingenuous speech about ending world hunger and bailing out those poor Wall Street firms. If the grass is dewy, good chance they'll slip and land on their *tuches*.

- Send anonymous, gift-wrapped boxes of your ashes to your most reviled officeholders. If they think it's after-the-bath talcum powder, imagine the places where you might land.

- Mail a package that has your ashes packed on the bottom and a few layers of dollar bills on top to the PAC or political party you despised the most, especially those folks who phoned you with those annoying fund-raising calls at dinnertime.

- Did your blood pressure go through the roof as you listened to those rabid radio pundits who tried to whip up their audiences with inflammatory right-or left wing inflammatory sound bites? A nice package to them with a note might get their attention; something like "wish this was you, not me."

77. Okay, You're Not Political—So Let's Light Up

Being a peace-and-love kind of person, maybe you find making a political statement way too extreme. Even getting you to vote has always seemed like a chore. Instead, you decide to meditate on some other options. That's when you realize that you can't meditate and chant "om" without a few candles burning. If you would like brighten your loved ones' lives, then how about becoming an essential ingredient in a votive candle? There are plenty of craft stores that can supply your friends with all they need.

Making these candles can even be part of your send-off service. What's more, you can choose a variety of scents that you always loved while air was still flowing in and out of your nose. Another idea is making birthday candles. Give them out to fifty people, and you are sure to be remembered at least fifty times a year, unless anyone you gave them to dies that year. (42)

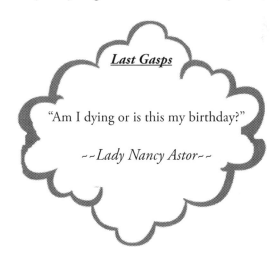

Last Gasps

"Am I dying or is this my birthday?"

~~Lady Nancy Astor~~

78. Finally Making Scents

If you buy into the candle thing, then why not throw in some incense sticks while you're at it? A mixture of you, gum Arabic, powdered sandalwood, some orrisroot, and the aromatic oil of your choice, and … *puff*, you are a joss stick for all your friends to inhale as a pungent memory no one will ever forget. Just hope that none of your friends has allergies. (43)

Did You Know

It was reported in the British magazine New Musical Express that Keith Richards snorted his father's ashes mixed with cocaine. The Rolling Stones guitarist, who has battled drug addiction, admits the ashes of his dad Bert were the strangest thing he ever sniffed. Richards later denied he did this.

---

79. Cleanliness Is Next to Godliness

Here's an over-the-top companion idea that requires a little ritual to go with it. Select the dearest and most intimate friends you left behind. After your service, have them receive a special gift basket containing (1) a framed picture of you, (2) one of those votive candles and a few joss sticks you had made, and (3) a new item that contains your essentials—a bar of "it's all about you" bath soap.

To make "your" soap, carefully choose a combination of quality oils, add your favorite fragrance, and swirl in a bubbly colorant. Then have one of your friends or family members add a dash or two of you. Presto, your soap unexpectedly takes on an unusual character that commercially made soaps can't even begin to compete with. Have these friends fill up the tub, light the candles, and slip into the soothing bath water, maybe with a nice glass of wine. As they lather up with you covering their bare essentials, they can gaze into the photograph, your eyes and smile twinkling at them—since you never saw them *au naturel* before. Or maybe you did. (44)

"Don't give me that "holier-than-thou" look!"

80. Youth Springs Eternal

You're converted to powder, wrinkles and all. But what about all those you left behind? How about giving them something to battle the aging process? You can, with a continuous moisturizing beauty cream. Infuse your friends' skin with moisture and a bit of you. Just have someone add a sprinkle of your ashes to any ultra-charged moisturizer that delivers skin-essential elements including zinc and manganese to keep skin hydrated all day. Your ashes are mostly calcium, a perfect add-in ingredient. Your parting gift will leave their skin glowing with health—unlike yours right now.

81. Rub It In

They didn't call you Magic Fingers for nothing. You loved to touch and be touched. Massages given and received were some of your most enjoyable experiences. For those people you touched or would still like to but never had the chance, you still can—even after you have ascended to that great massage parlor in the sky. Have your send-off team take pinches of your powdery residue and add it to small bottles of massage oil. Have them distributed to everyone you ever fantasized about. Just imagine the hot places where you might wind up.

Quotable Quotes

"The secret of staying young is to live honestly, eat slowly, and lie about your age."

~~Lucille Ball~~
(1911–1989)

---

82. X-Rated Suggestions Will Not Be Mentioned in This Book

I thought about a section devoted to what you could do with your ashes in terms of self-pleasure toys, nude beaches, and suppositories. But I decided that would reduce this book to a deplorable level that would insult and offend the sensibilities of my distinguished readers.

"Just because I tossed a bit of Mother's ashes under our bed doesn't mean our sex life is over."

83. Do Yourself a Flavor

Now that you have figured out how to get yourself into soap, candles, incense, massage oil, and sex toys (maybe you have some of your own ideas), you need to focus on feeding those intimates of yours since by now they've worked up an appetite that could kill a cow (or a slab of tofu, for the vegetarians in your group).

You've already been incinerated, so why not repeat that experience with a tasty grand finale for your pals. How, you ask? By turning your remains into savory, spiced-up barbeque briquettes that can be used at the family's next Fourth of July gathering. Forget about mesquite or hickory woodchips to add flavor to those hamburgers, steaks, and chicken breasts. Let the smoky aroma of your fundamental essence add spice and a unique seasoning to the victuals. This will be one pig-out that will go down in history and up in smoke. (45)

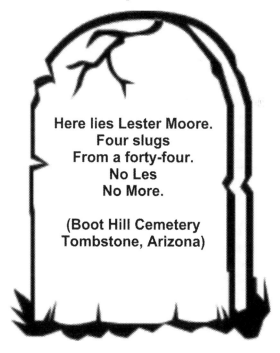

Here lies Lester Moore.
Four slugs
From a forty-four.
No Les
No More.

(Boot Hill Cemetery
Tombstone, Arizona)

XIV. More Than Fifteen Minutes of Fame

We know that you always got weak-kneed over celebrities and secretly wished you had become one. You fantasized about all that adulation and money you could have had. More important, if you had made it, you wouldn't have had your mother pestering you all the time about what a disappointment you were to the entire family.

Well, you didn't make it, and your mother was right. The next-best thing at this point would be getting interred next to someone who did make it, was famous, and was a household name. Don't fret, because now you can. Here's how.

84. Cozy Up with the Famous

We established that you loved them from a distance. The movie stars, musicians, the rich and the famous. You may not have been able to get close to them in life, but you can in death with some creative scattering. All you need to do is find out where they are buried, and have your team spread your ashes about these celebrities' graves. You can find out where many of Hollywood's nobility and others of the world's greatest are buried by going to the Web. Try www.findagrave.com and www.hollywood-underground.com/departed. (46)

Did You Know

According to morbid-curiosity.com, Truman Capote, who died in Joanna Carson's home (the ex–Mrs. Johnny Carson), was cremated. His ashes split between Joanna and his lover. Carson kept the ashes at her home in Bel Air. One Halloween, during a costume party, they were stolen. Six nights later, a mysterious car dropped off the ashes, leaving them in a coiled-up garden hose. Carson feared the remaining ashes could be stolen again and bought Capote a crypt for his cremains at Westwood Memorial Park, near his friends Marilyn Monroe and Natalie Wood.

---

85. Hard and Hardly Famous

As a starry-eyed fan of Hollywood's finest, you might think about something other than getting strewn around someone's grave. That's when you think about getting your ashes mixed into the cement they use at Grauman's Chinese Theatre in Hollywood. You might remember that this famous collection of footprints and handprints began with an accident. Rumor has it that before the theater officially opened, the owner gave a tour to some celebrities, at which point actress Norma Talmadge unintentionally walked across a wet slab of cement.

Variations of this honored tradition are imprints of the cigars of Groucho Marx and George Burns, Betty Grable's legs, John Wayne's fist, and the noses of Jimmy Durante and Bob Hope. Just pray that a once-famous pet (à la Lassie, Flicker, or Old Yeller—or a porn star) isn't selected for an impression when your batch hardens. (47)

86. Give Your Regards to Broadway

You loved the Great White Way, the plays, the stars, and the pulse of the Big Apple. From Ziegfeld to Pinter, great theater took place on these lively streets that the Muses smiled upon. Want to give your final regards to Broadway? Ethel Merman did it, so why not you? Just have your team rent a big limo—or, better yet, an old Cadillac convertible—and let your ashes fly up and over the lighted marquees as you zip through Times Square. Not a bad final act.

<u>Did You Know</u>

According to Karen Kramer in the New York Times, Damon Runyon, famous newspaperman and writer, had his friend Eddie Rickenbacker, the World War I flying ace, fulfill Runyon's wish to have his ashes scattered over Broadway and did so from the cockpit of an airplane in 1946.

"They say Eddy's last act was unforgettable."

XV. Being a Good Sport

From Roman gladiators battling it to the death to twenty-first-century fans getting peptic ulcers every time the World Series rolls around, sports have been a big part of life, especially yours. Why not pick out an appropriate way to commemorate your *fanaticism* by choosing the sport that resonates with you the most?

87. The People in the Bleachers Will Love You

You loved your team and will miss them sorely now that you are gone. So, why not stay close to them forever? It's easy enough to get a tour of your favorite baseball park or football stadium. Have your designated team members keep you in their pockets and make sure their pockets have holes in them. Have them stroll down the baselines and end up at home plate, leaving your spirited remains along the way.

You loved football? Then how about something dropped around the goal posts or on the gridiron? Soccer fields and golf courses are also possibilities. Clay and grass tennis courts are a snap. Basketball courts may offer a challenge unless you can get the maintenance crew to toss you into their floor wax. If ice hockey was your thing, then get the Zamboni guy who resurfaces the ice to mix your ashes into the water that they use at halftime to smooth out the skating-rink dings.

"Cousin Vinny was a big fan of yours so I buried his ashes under your mound."

Did You Know
It is rumored that Harpo Marx has his ashes strewn around the sand trap at the seventh hole of Rancho Mirage's golf course.
Humorist Lewis Grizzard had his ashes planted on the fifty-yard line at Sanford Stadium at the University of Georgia.

88. The One That Got Away

They say you always wanted to be remembered as a great sports fisherman or -woman. You reeled in a few good ones, but there was that one big one that got away. Here's another chance to redeem yourself. Direct your executors to have your memorial service on a fishing party boat. Make sure the captain knows the fishing grounds, particularly where to find the lunkers. Have the boat motor out to the best spot, and whoever officiates the service can offer a blessing to the people on the boat and a prayer for a great catch of the day. Have the bait everyone uses dipped into your ashes. Cast off those lines, and have faith that someone lands the big Kahuna. With those tasty ashes, how can Charlie the Tuna resist? When the boat returns, have that fish taxidermied and mounted with a plaque in honor of you. Who gets to keep the trophy fish is another story.

Quotable Quotes

"Fishing is a delusion entirely surrounded by liars in old clothes."

--Don Marquis--
(1878–1937)

---

89. The Big Dusting

If you want to really mingle with fans and stadiums, then think crop duster. Imagine Super Bowl Sunday, the World Series, the Masters Tournament, the French Open, or the Olympics. Hire a courageous and stealthy pilot to swing over your favorite event and let your dustings fly. Players and fans will breathe you in with joy. The gridiron grass, tennis lawns, or outfield sod wouldn't be too upset with the extra sustenance you offer, either.

Did You Know

Misty May-Treanor, gold medalist at the 2008 Olympics in Beijing for beach volleyball, has scattered her mom's ashes at every tournament she has won including the 2004 Olympics in Athens.

---

90. A More Intimate Dusting

I haven't forgotten you indoor sports junkies who love basketball, volleyball, bowling, or ping-pong. Fill a few helium balloons with your ashes, let them go inside the arena, and then have your best pea-shooter friends (a BB gun will do if you can smuggle one in) puncture them when they are high above the roaring crowds. Your ashes will rain down, showering one and all with your love.

91. Giddy Up

The mother of a friend of mine loved to go to the races. When she passed, he took her ashes and sprinkled them at Belmont. If you like the idea, here are ten famous racetracks to bet your ash on:

- Churchill Downs (Louisville, Kentucky), site of the Kentucky Derby
- Aqueduct (Queens, New York)
- Beulah Park (Grove City, Ohio)
- Del Mar (Del Mar, California)
- Saratoga (Saratoga Springs, New York)
- Santa Rosa (Santa Rosa, California)
- Suffolk Downs (East Boston, Massachusetts)
- Pimlico (Laurel, Maryland)
- Meadowlands (East Rutherford, New Jersey)
- Santa Anita (Arcadia, California)

Quotable Quotes

"I bet on a horse at ten to one. It didn't come in until half-past five."

~~Henny Youngman~~
(1906-1998)

---

92. When Powder Meets Powder

Remember the thrills and spills you had skiing down those adrenaline-pumping ski slopes? The views were spectacular. The air was fresh and invigorating. Those moguls and black ice made you want to scootch in your cool-looking three-layer, four-way stretch twill, waterproof, breathable membrane ski pants.

So how about laying your powder on your favorite downhill powder? Killington, Vail, Big Sky, or even Davos and the Alps. Just have your farewell ski party lead the way and schuss down the fall line. With the lid off the urn or whatever container you choose (your old ski boot may do), the wind will take your powder for the ride of your life. If you happen to pass away off-season, have your party take you to the top of the mountain on the ski lift and scatter you along the way.

> *Quotable Quotes*
>
> *"Skiing combines outdoor fun with knocking down trees with your face."*
>
> ~~Dave Barry~~

93. Bambi Will Hate You, and So Will My Kid

I am not a big fan of hunting warm-blooded things with fur and eyelids that blink. But if I say it's open season on fish, it would be hypocritical to say that Disney creatures are off limits. This time, get your hunting buddies to storm off into the woods with ammo they've made with cartridges containing a mixture of gunpowder, lead, and you. They can do the mounted-trophy thing like with the fish. They can also cook up whatever innocent creature had no chance in hell of escaping with your hunting pals using Dragunov sniper rifles equipped with scopes.

A good hunter always eats what he beats, so have a real party. Sprinkle a dash of ash on the open-pit fire and maybe a dusting of you on the creature you bagged. And make the guy that actually bagged the beast eat the prairie oysters. *¡Muy macho!*

Quotable Quotes

"Stuffed deer heads on walls are bad enough, but it's worse when they are wearing dark glasses and have streamers and ornaments in their antlers because then you know they were enjoying themselves at a party when they were shot."

~~Ellen DeGeneres~~

---

94. Lucky Lanes

If you were a bowler with one of those shirts with your name stitched over the pocket, you can still get a strike from the next world. See if you can make arrangements with a company that makes custom bowling balls, and have them add you to their pro-rubber formula. Donate the ball to your favorite bowling lane where lots of people will hook you down the alley. Or hand down the ball to your kids or grandchildren, and have them celebrate your birthday at the lanes. You can also have holes drilled into the bowling pins with your ashes poured in. Spare nothing.

95. Minnesota Fats

Same idea as the bowling ball, only this time you get to be incorporated into fifteen pool balls (sixteen if you include the cue ball). Just think—dead balls and kill shots will have a whole new meaning now. You can be cast into the resin of pool balls that are marbleized, glow in the dark, are pearlescent, or are traditional style. If your ashes have to be drilled into holes, you can count on having loopy shots. But since you and your buddies probably stank at pool anyway, no one will notice. Or if they do, they can blame it on you.

96. A Dimpled Approach

We're not talking about those cute dimples you might have had on your face. We're talking about the game of chili dipping, thinning, topping, slicing, duck hooks, flop shots, and jelly legs. That's right—the game of golf. So what if you were never that good? Nobody is, unless the stars are aligned properly and Ben Hogan is smiling down on you. But the game is addictive, and if you had been buried the old-fashioned way, you would have opted for some casket space *under* the eighteenth green at Pebble Beach or Saint Andrews. (Of course, you can still be scattered *over* the courses of your choosing like Harpo.)

Well, one way of staying on course above ground is to add your ashes to a set of custom-made balata-covered balls. Give the balls away to your golfing foursome (threesome now), donate them to the PGA tour, or send them to Tiger. The next hole anyone gets with you inside will be truly divine.

Last Gasps

"That was a great game of golf, fellers."

~~Bing Crosby~~

97. Take a Hike

Hitting those trails and backpacking through the White Mountains, along the Appalachian Trail, or down the Pacific Crest put you at one with nature and the world. You and your hiking stick were best pals, since it helped keep your balance, gave you better maneuverability, and, best of all, saved your lower back and creaky knees. So why not have a hole drilled down the stick's middle to hold your ashes? Pass that stick along to someone in your family who loves hiking as much as you did. Just make sure they don't use it for roasting marshmallows.

"Do me a big favor Joe, dump me into all your top shelf booze when I go to that big distillery in the sky."

XVI. Leaving It to Chance and to Others

At this point, you've read quite a few different ways to dispose of your ashes. Maybe you are thinking that all this is too challenging a task. You've read these brilliant ideas and you still can't make up your mind. Your head aches at all the different locations and ways you could be scattered, buried, urned, and interred. So if you're the type that always passed the buck to others all your life—come on, admit it—then why not now? Once again, you can have other people figure things out for you. Why not give them your ashes and leave what happens to you up to chance?

98. A Message in a Bottle

Perhaps that idea of chance is actually intriguing to you. You toyed with a burial at sea, but it lacked adventure. You don't want to plunge to the ocean floor and just sit there like the hulk of a rusting oil barge, or get scattered on the ocean's surface and dissolve like a thin sheet of frothy soap detergent.

Then why not choose a corked bottle as your urn! Just get yourself poured inside, have a mysterious note placed inside, have it tossed into the ocean, and get carried away by the currents to who knows where—Tahiti, Madagascar, Aruba, maybe Staten Island. Then think of that beautiful young woman or man walking on the beach around sunrise who finds you, places the bottle in a sacred place, and passes you on from one generation to the next. Or as luck may have it, they drop you into the recycling bin.

"Says, "We hope that Aunt Clara has found her way to a very exotic land overflowing with excitement and interesting people."

99. Bag It and Pass It

Here's a way to leave to others the responsibility of both *how* and *where* your ashes wind up. At your funeral, have your ashes put into tasteful sachet bags for people to scatter as they wish. Think of them as party favors. Have enough bags for what you guess will be the number of bereaved guests you hope will show up, and have the bags handed out after the service is over. Instruct the mourners to conduct their own private farewell rituals.

The beauty of the sachet giveaway is that you can have a hundred different rituals take place to honor you, assuming you have that many friends show up. You'll have more memorial services than ten cats have lives. Better yet, your essence will be spread in more places than God has sinners. Of course, some of your supposed friends might just toss you out the car window right after they leave the chapel. But hey, life is one really long ride on Fate's unpredictable highway. And maybe that eight-wheeler that just ran over the sachet bag is going to New Orleans. You always wanted to visit the French Quarter during Mardi Gras.

> *Quotable Quotes*
>
> *"No matter how rich you become, how famous or powerful, when you die the size of your funeral will still pretty much depend on the weather.*
>
> ~~Michael Pritchard~~

100. Take a Scenic Route

So maybe that sachet thing didn't spark your interest. But you like the idea of casting your fate to the wind but prefer something a bit more off-beat. Why not try the Hobo Walkabout? Have your ashes placed in a suitcase and left randomly on a train, a Trailways bus, or container ship headed to Asia. You get to travel to some unknown destination, and who knows what will happen at the end of the road? Who said you had no sense of adventure!

> *Quotable Quotes*
>
> *"Thanks to the Interstate Highway System, it is now possible to travel from coast to coast without seeing anything."*
>
> ~~Charles Kuralt~~
> (1934–1997)

101. A Test of Character

Here's another idea if you like the thrill of something daring, unpredictable, and random. Take a suitcase again—but this time a classy one—and have someone leave it on a busy street corner, preferably in a big city with lots of pedestrians. Seal your ashes tightly in antique candlesticks and put them in the suitcase. Will some honest soul turn you in to the lost and found, where you will spend eternity (yech)? Or will some felonious character smuggle you to their home and display you on their dining table to impress guests? Then again, you just might wind up at an auction at Sotheby's or, by another turn of events, in a pawnshop.

102. Let Your Fingers Do the Walking

For something really random, why not take a phone book, any phone book, and randomly pick a name? Choose a city you never visited, somewhere you always wanted to go. Send your ashes, priority mail. Include a note, or not.

Did You Know

According to the Associated Press, cremation ashes were found inside a package placed in a mail collection box. The letter carrier found the package wrapped haphazardly in a plastic bag, with no mailing or return address, and notified police. A police dog did not detect any explosives, so officers opened it and found a box with a metal plate with the deceased person's name on it and the years "1957–2000."

---

103. Polar Express Yourself

Do you still believe in Santa? Well, it doesn't really matter now. But if you want to make an "I still believe, I still believe" statement, then have them pack up your ashes and send them

UPS to Santa with a letter. (First, figure out if your life has been naughty or nice.) If you believe, then you will definitely wind up as talcum powder for the elves to soothe their tired little hands from making all those play-with-once, forget-about tomorrow toys. But remember, if you're wrong and there really is no Santa, you might (1) end up in the dead-letter bin, (2) get sent to a local charity who will try and answer your letter, or (3) get burned with all the other Santa letters. If you wind up with option three, you'll get a double cremation, but this one will only cost you the price of priority mail.

Quotable Quotes

"I stopped believing in Santa Claus when my mother took me to see him in a department store, and he asked me for my autograph."

~~Shirley Temple~~

---

104. Highest Bidder

How much are you really worth? Not much, once you are cremated. But now you have a chance to be the object of a fierce bidding war. All you need is an expensive collectable or antique in which your ashes will be placed. Instruct your executor to put you on eBay with no reserve. Where and with you whom you wind up is anyone's guess. And what they do after that, who knows? The proceeds from your sale will make your estate very happy. Who said you were a good-for-nothing?

Brian thought Grandma Minnie's urn might fetch a good price on eBay.

105. Okay, Just Forget About It

You can scream hallelujah because at last you have reached the end of the road of ways to deal with your ashes. If, in spite of everything you read, you are at a loss and are still racking your brain about cool ways to get rid of your timeless leftovers, here is one last idea.

We can all agree on one thing. You are cremated. The funeral folks have your ashes all gathered up and deposited in a plastic container waiting for your family to pick you up. Well, don't have anyone show up! Sure, the funeral director might try and call your daughter-in-law who was kind enough to take care of the arrangements, but she gave them the phone number of the Chinese restaurant you loved to eat at just like you requested. What they do with you is anyone's guess. Maybe it's better that way.

"That's All Folks!"
The Man of a
Thousand Voices

~~Mel Blanc~~

Thanks for taking time to read this book. *See you in the next life.*

APPENDIX A – Sources and Resources

I have listed a number of Web site links to access resources mentioned in this book. This is not an exhaustive list, and you may find some links no longer active. However, you can find additional resources and information on your own by using some of the popular search engines like Google and Yahoo. Just type in a key word, for example "cremation services" or "ash scattering" and you will find many web sites filled with information.

1.   Funeralplan.com
www.funeralplan.com/funeralplan/cremation/stats.html
www.cremationassociation.org/html/statistics.html

2.   Cremation Association of America
www.cremationassociation.org/html/history.html

3.   Cremation Association of America
www.cremationassociation.org/html/history.html

4.   Cremation Association of America
www.cremationassociation.org/html/history.html

5.   *Purified by Fire: A History of Cremation in America* by Stephen R. Prothero

6.   Cremationinfo.com
www.cremationinfo.com/cremationinfo/Questions.htm

7.   Yolo County Sheriff's Department Coroner
www.yolocountysheriff.com/coroner_questions.htm

8.   Funerals with Love
www.funeralswithlove.com/funeralcosts.htm

9.   A few Web sites you can peruse for urns
www.classicurns.com/
www.cremationurnfactory.com/
www.prestigememorials.com/
www.zigzagurns.com/

10.   From Wikipedia
(en.wikipedia.org/wiki/Green_burial)—Compiled from statistics by Casket and Funeral Association of America, Cremation Association of North America, Doric Inc., The Rainforest Action Network, and Mary Woodsen, Pre-Posthumous Society. To find green burial sites, search the Web with the keywords "green burial cemeteries" or "green burials."

11.   Scattering gardens
www.natureschapel.com
Also, search the Web for "scattering gardens"

12.   Memorial rocks
Everlife Memorials
www.everlifememorials.com/garden-memorials-rocks-catalog.htm
Prestige Memorials
www.prestigememorials.com/memorial-rocks.php

13.   Statues and art options
Classic Memorials
www.classicmemorials.com/memorial-statues.htm

Art in Ashes
www.artinashes.com/Cremation-Artists-information.php

Cast your ashes in stone sculpture
Ashes into Stone
www.ashesinstone.com/index.html

Other options:
Search the Web for "cast stone sculpture"
and ask about adding your ashes

There are many companies that memorialize pets; ask if they would do the same for your ashes.

14.   Waterfalls
Just go to your favorite Web search engine (Google, Yahoo, etc.), and key in "prefabricated waterfalls." Call any of the matches you get, and ask how they feel about putting your ashes in their next batch of waterfall mix.
www.rock-n-water.com/
www.rockwaterdesigns.com/aboutus.htm
www.backyardxscapes.com/waterfalls/waterfalls.html

15.   Time capsules
www.ridgequest.co.uk/Timecapsules.htm
www.heritagetimecapsules.com
www.futurepkg.com

16.   Sculptors
Resources related to sculptors and sculpture on and off the Internet:
www.sculptor.org/
List of links to the websites of sculptor's original works.
http://dir.webring.com/rw
(search "Sculptors)
Canadian sculptors
www.cansculpt.org

17. Urns
A Complete Guide to Choosing Urns Online
www.classicurns.com
Websites for urns:
www.faster-results.com/us.fastuk/search/web/Cremation-Urns/
www.google.com/Top/Shopping/Death_Care/Urns/
www.dmoz.org/Shopping/Death_Care/Urns
www.theurnist.com
www.michaelorgelsculpture.com/urns-portfolio.htm

18. Wooden Urns
www.mainelyurns.com/hardwood-urns.html
www.mabreyproducts.com
www.bergstrom.ee
www.phoenixurn.com/gpage4.html
www.deansurns.com

19. Fabric Urns
www.renaissanceurns.com/pages/fabric.htm
www.funeral-urn.com
www.mycremationurns.com/site/1400820/page/561710
www.cremationkeepsakes.com/urns.htm

20. Sculpture and art urns
In the Light Urns
www.inthelighturns.com/sculpture.html
Crematory Urns
www.crematoryurns.com/crematory_urns_bronze.html

21.   Sports Theme Urns
Everlife Memorials
www.everlifememorials.com/urns-catalog.htm
Kelco
www.kelcosupply.com/infinity/d005p236.html
Cremation Urns of Vermont
www.cremationurnsofvermont.com/sportsurns.html
Prestige Memorials
www.prestigememorials.com/

22.   Hobby Urns
Prestige Memorials
http://www.prestigememorials.com/Urns-Hobby-Urns-
information.php
Huggable Urns
http://www.huggableurns.com/testimonials.php

23.   Scattering at Sea
Ashes on the Sea (www.ashesonthesea.com)
Pacific Coast Ashes At Sea (www.cremainsatsea.com)
Love Hawaii (www.lovehawaii.com/ashes.html)
Note: For more at sea options, search the Web using keywords
   "Burial at Sea" and "Scattering at Sea"

24.   Memorial Reefs
www.eternalreefs.com
www.greatburialreef.com
www.nmreef.com

25.   Fireworks and You
Zambelli Fireworks Packed Hunter Thompson's ashes into a
display: www.zambellifireworks.com/home.html
Angel's Flight
www.angels-flight.net
Note: For more fireworks options, search the Web using keywords
"Firework Displays"

26. Scattering by Air

A partial list of aerial scattering services:

Aerial Missions

www.aerialmissions.com

Cloud-Nine Coastal Flights

(www.cloud9flights.com)

Four Winds Aerial Scattering

(www.fourwindsaerial.com)

Wing and a Prayer

(www.wingandaprayer.net)

Note: For more aerial scattering options, search the Web using keywords "scattering by air" and "aerial ash scattering"

27. Ballon Ascent

Eternal Ascent

www.eternalascent.com/index.html

28. Launch Your Ashes into Space

Memorial Space Flights

www.memorialspaceflights.com

Starburst Memorials

www.columbiad.ca/starburst/index.html

29. Shipping Your Ashes

You can ship ashes following United States Postal Service (USPS) guidelines. Currently, Federal Express and UPS do not offer shipping services. The USPS guidelines for shipping can be found by going to this publication: www.usps.com/cpim/ftp/pubs/pub52.pdf

30. Piñata sources

www.pinatas.com/ (you can buy them here)

www.kinderplanet.com/pinata.htm (or learn how to make one)

31. Punching Bags

www.everlastboxing.com/

www.9thstreetgym.com/

32.   Disney information
disneyland.disney.go.com/

33.   Las Vegas Chamber of Commerce
www.lvchamber.com/index.htm

34.   US National Parks information
www.nps.gov/
www.us-national-parks.net/

35.   Diamonds Forever
www.lifegem.com/

36.   Then There's Costume Jewelry
www.jewelrykeepsakes.com
www.perfectmemorials.com
www.prestigememorials.com

37.   Graffiti Artist Information
www.graffiti.org/

38.   Making Crayons
familycrafts.about.com/cs/craftsupplies/ht/RecycledCrayon.htm
www.fresnofamily.com/activities/crayons.htm
www.stresslesscountry.com/making-new-crayons/index.html

39.   Making Kitchen Magnets
www.make-stuff.com/projects/wallpaper_accessories.html
www.creativegeek.com/magnet.shtml

40.   Dyeing Resources
www.dharmatrading.com/dyes/
www.wildflowerdyes.com/howtotiedye.html
jas.familyfun.go.com/crafts?page=CraftDisplay&craftid=11004

41.   Custom-Made Bells
www.bronzebells.com/
www.imakebells.com

42.   Candlemaking
www.candlewic.com/default.asp
www.candletech.com/
www.pioneerthinking.com/candles.html
www.cierracandles.com/

43.   Making Incense
www.oller.net/incense-making.htm
www.scents-of-earth.com/makyourownna.html
www.makeincense.com/
www.jmw.net/how_to_make_incense.html

44.   Soap Making
waltonfeed.com/old/soaphome.html
candleandsoap.about.com/
www.kidsdomain.com/craft/easysoap.html

45.   BBQ Briquette Making
www.shop.edirectory.co.uk/easylifeonline/pages/moreinfoa.asp?
pe=CCEJGIFQ_+briquette+maker&cid=1649
www.taylorgifts.com/prodetail.asp?src=FRGL0406&itemno=27
931&CAWELAID=146564019

46.   Cozy Up With the Famous
www.seeing-stars.com/Buried/index.shtml
www.findagrave.com
www.hollywoodusa.co.uk/celebrity-graves.htm
www.gravehunter.net/index.html

47.   Grauman's Chinese Theatre: Footprint Ceremonies
www.manntheatres.com/chinese/ceremonies.php

APPENDIX B – Flamed and Famous

Most people who are cremated and for that matter most people in general live and die anonymously. To illustrate the popularity of cremation by those that lived as celebrities, here is a partial list of famous people who decided to be cremated.

- Bud Abbott (actor; part of Abbott and Costello comedy team)

- Ansel Adams (famous outdoor photographer)

- June Allyson (a Golden Globe–winning American film and television actress popular in the 1940s and 1950s)

- Dana Andrews (American film actor who starred in *The Ox-Bow Incident*, *Where the Sidewalk Ends*, and in the Oscar-winning 1946 film *The Best Years of Our Lives*.)

- Don Ameche (actor popular in the '40s and a star in *Cocoon*)

- Fatty Arbuckle (actor falsely accused of rape; was exonerated but career was ruined)

- Desi Arnaz (married to Lucille Ball and star of *I Love Lucy*)

- Jean Arthur (actress who played wife in *Shane*)

- Isaac Asimov (scientist and master of the science-fiction genre)

- Ingrid Bergman (actress who jilted Bogie in *Casablanca*)

- Bill Bixby (*My Favorite Martian* actor)

- Amanda Blake (actress who played Kitty on *Gunsmoke*)

- Beulah Bondi (a veteran actress who worked well into her 80s, best remembered for her role as Mrs. Bailey, the mother of George Bailey, in *It's a Wonderful Life*.

- Richard Boone (*Have Gun, Will Travel* star)

- Humphrey Bogart (do we need to say more)

- Marlon Brando (ditto Stella)

- Lloyd Bridges (blub, blub, blub actor who starred in many land and underwater movies and the TV series *Sea Hunt*)

- William F. Buckley (American author, conservative commentator, and founder of *National Review* in 1955, who hosted the television show *Firing Line*. Known as a nationally syndicated newspaper columnist whose writing style was famed for its erudition, wit, and use of uncommon words.)

- Red Buttons (Oscar-winning actor for his role in *Sayonara*, he performed in numerous feature films, including *Hatari!*, *The Longest Day*, *Harlow*, *The Poseidon Adventure*, and *They Shoot Horses, Don't They?*)

- Rory Calhoun (tough guy actor starring in more than eighty motion pictures and a large number of television episodes.)

- Truman Capote (well-dressed novelist and author of *In Cold Blood.*)

- George Carlin (groundbreaking stand-up comedian noted for attacking social taboos)

- John Carradine (actor in movies including *Grapes of Wrath* and *Bride of Frankenstein*)

- Johnny Carson (best late night talk show host ever)

- Jack Cassidy (American actor, who achieved success in theater, cinema and television.)

- Wilt Chamberlain (NBA Hall of Fame center nicknamed Wilt the Stilt.)

- Lou Chaney Jr. (renowned horror movie actor)

- Kurt Cobain (singer and guitarist for Nirvana)

- James Coburn (star of *Our Man Flint* and *The Magnificent Seven*)

- Imogene Coca (Sid Caesar's side-splitting comedy partner)

- Wally Cox (actor who starred on television and movies with a screen persona of a shy, timid but kind man who wore thick eyeglasses and spoke in a pedantic, high-pitched voice.)

- Richard Crenna (American actor with a long career in films, appearing in such movies as *The Sand Pebbles, Wait Until Dark, Body Heat,* and *First Blood.)*

- Bob Cummings (of TV's *Love That Bob* show)

- Bobby Darin (one of the most popular American big band performers and rock and roll teen idols of the late 1950s with hits like "Dream Lover," "Beyond the Sea," and "Mack the Knife.")

- Linda Darnell (American film actress with starring roles in *Blood and Sand, Hangover Square,* and *My Darling Clementine.*)

- Ossie Davis (one of the notable African American actors and directors of his generation. Films in which he starred in included *Do The Right Thing, Jungle Fever, Grumpy Old Men,* and *I'm Not Rappaport.*)

- Yvonne De Carlo (Canadian-born American film and television actress, best known for her role as Lily Munster on the 1964–1966 CBS television series *The Munsters.*)

- John Denver (famous folksy singer with hits like "Rocky Mountain High.")

- Walt Disney (Mickey's dad)

- Andy Devine (actor with a very peculiar voice who hosted *Andy's Gang,* played Jingles, and appeared in over 400 movies.)

- Margaret Dumont (dowager comic foil to Groucho Marx in seven of the Marx Brothers movies. Groucho called her practically the fifth Marx brother.)

- Madelyn Payne Dunham (President Barack Obama's grandmother)

- Albert Einstein ($E = mc^2$)

- George Fenneman (announcer on the Groucho Marx quiz show, *You Bet Your Life.*)

- Henry Fonda (*On Golden Pond* actor and father of Jane.)

- Greta Garbo ("I vant to be alone" actress.)

- Jerry Garcia (lead guitarist and singer of the Grateful Dead.)

- Will Geer (played Grandpa Walton on *The Waltons.*)

- Maurice Gibb (Bee Gees singer)

- Robert Giroux (editor and publisher of Farrar, Straus & Giroux who introduced and nurtured some of the major authors of the twentieth century)

- Ruth Gordon (actress and star in cult classic *Harold and Maude.*)

- Cary Grant (debonair leading man in movies such as *North by Northwest, Bringing Up Baby, The Philadelphia Story*, and *Gunga Din.*)

- George Harrison (guitarist, singer, songwriter and sitar player of the Beatles.)

- Rex Harrison (suave British actor best known for his role as Professor Higgins in *My Fair Lady.*)

- Phil Hartman (known for his impressions as a regular on *Saturday Night Live*, this talented actor and comedian met an untimely death, murdered by his wife.)

- Charlton Heston (Academy Award winning actor best remembered for his roles in *The Ten Commandments* and *Ben-Hur*, as well as president of the National Rifle Association)

- Sir Edmund Hillary (Mount Everest climber, who asked that his ashes be scattered on Auckland's Waitemata Harbor, "to complete the cycle of my life.")

- Alfred Hitchcock (famed film director and producer of suspense thriller films like *Psycho, The Birds, North by Northwest*, and many others.)

- William Holden (Academy Award-winning American film actor, starring in films like *Golden Boy, Our Town, Sunset*

Boulevard, The Bridges at Toko-Ri, Love Is a Many-Splendored Thing, and *The Wild Bunch.*)

- Rock Hudson (good-looking romantic lead, he was the first actor to announce he had contracted AIDS.)

- Walter Huston (American actor who starred in *Duel in the Sun* and *The Treasure of the Sierra Madre,* in which he won an Academy Award.)

- Jill Ireland (actress who had her ashes made into a walking stick for her husband, Charles Bronson.)

- Henry James (famous American novelist with works including *Daisy Miller, Washington Square,* and *The Turn of the Screw.*)

- Van Johnson (well-known actor who starred in *Pal Joey, Thirty Seconds Over Tokyo, Battleground,* and *The Caine Mutiny.*)

- Janis Joplin (hard-living, feisty rock singing member of Big Brother and the Holding Company.)

- Hamilton Jordan (a chief strategist for President Jimmy Carter. After Carter's victory, Jordan became chief of staff.)

- Howard Keel (American actor who starred in many classic film musicals of the 1950s as well as oil baron Clayton Farlow in the TV series *Dallas.*)

- Helen Keller (deaf and blind American author, activist, and lecturer.)

- Gene Kelly (famed dancer, choreographer, and actor who starred in *For Me and My Gal, Singin' in the Rain, Pal Joey,* and *An American in Paris.*)

- DeForest Kelley (played Dr. "Bones" McCoy on *Star Trek.*)

- John F. Kennedy Jr.(who died in a tragic plane crash along with his wife Carolyn and her sister Lauren, all cremated.)

- Roland Kirk (avant-garde jazz musician who said "When I die I want them to play 'The Black and Crazy Blues,' I want to be cremated, put in a bag of pot and I want beautiful people to smoke me and hope they get something out of it.")

- Veronica Lake (popular American film actress and pin-up model who enjoyed both popular and critical acclaim, especially for her femme fatale roles in film noir with Alan Ladd during the 1940s.)

- Fernando Lamas (Billy Crystal had fun with his "You look MAHHHHvelous" shtick; however, Lamas was an established movie star in Argentina who went to the United States to play "Latin Lover" roles.)

- Hope Lange (*Peyton Place* actress)

- Yves Saint Laurent (famous high-fashion designer)

- Peter Lawford (English-born Hollywood actor, member of Frank Sinatra's "Rat Pack," and brother-in-law to John F. Kennedy.)

- Timothy Leary (1960s counterculture writer, psychologist, and advocate of the therapeutic and spiritual benefits of LSD.)

- Heath Ledger (Oscar nominee whose films include *Dark Night, Brokeback Mountain, Monster's Ball,* and *A Knight's Tale*)

- Vivian Leigh (starred as Scarlett O'Hara and Blanche DuBois, winning two Oscars despite a twenty-year marriage to Sir Laurence Olivier including bouts of hysteria and depression, an affair with Peter Finch, and her peculiar "poetic" nervousness.)

- John Lennon (murdered rock icon and peace activist, singer, songwriter, and guitarist for the Beatles.)

- Shari Lewis (popular puppeteer and creator of Lamb Chop, the lovable sock puppet.)

- Miriam Makeba (South African music legend)

- Henry Mancini (noted composer of theme songs for movies like *Breakfast at Tiffany's, The Pink Panther,* and *Charade.*)

- Maharishi Mahesh Yogi (spiritual leader of Transcendental Meditation who took the technique to the West, gaining fame when he introduced it to the Beatles in 1968.)

- Harpo Marx (the Marx brother who never spoke, nicknamed Harpo because he played the harp.)

- Groucho Marx (wisecracking, hustling comedian with a unique chicken-walking lope and exaggerated greasepaint mustache, who loved to insult stuffy dowagers and anyone else who stood in his way)

- Freddie Mercury (lead singer of Queen who died of AIDS.)

- Burgess Meredith (adept playing both dramatic and comedic roles in films including *Rocky*, *Grumpy Old Men*, and *Batman*.)

- Ethel Merman (star of stage and film musicals, well known for her powerful belting voice and vocal range.)

- Harvey Milk (first openly gay American politician to be elected in California; later assassinated along with San Francisco Mayor Moscone by a disgruntled city supervisor.)

- Henry Miller (American writer best known for his works *Tropic of Cancer*, *Tropic of Capricorn*, and *Black Spring*.)

- Charles Mingus (ranked among the finest composers and performers in jazz, he was bassist, bandleader, and occasional pianist.)

- Robert Mitchum (pot-smoking actor who starred in major works of the film noir genre, and considered a forerunner of the antiheroes prevalent in films during the 1950s and '60s.)

- Joel McCrea (handsome leading man who starred in more than a dozen Westerns.)

- Roddy McDowell (child actor who had a successful adult career with movies like *Planet of the Apes*, *A Bug's Life*, and *Poseidon Adventure*.)

- Steve McQueen (his breakout role in TV's Western series *Wanted: Dead or Alive* led McQueen to roles in *The Magnificent Seven*, *Bullitt*, *Sand Pebbles*, and *The Great Escape*.)

- Barry Morse (actor who played a detective pursuing the wrongly accused Dr. Richard Kimble in 1960s TV series *The Fugitive*)

- Edward R. Murrow (prominent news broadcaster during World War II, and one of journalism's greatest figures—Murrow was noted for honesty and integrity. A pioneer of television news broadcasting, Murrow filed reports that helped lead to the censure Senator Joseph McCarthy.)

- Paul Newman (beloved Oscar winner and philanthropist who starred in *Butch Cassidy and the Sundance Kid, Cool Hand Luke, The Sting*, and many others.)

- Georgia O'Keeffe (American artist and wife of photographer Alfred Stieglitz, O'Keeffe is widely regarded as one of the greatest painters of the twentieth century.)

- Dorothy Parker (American writer and poet best known for her caustic wit, wisecracks, and sharp eye for twentieth-century urban foibles.)

- Anthony Perkins (American actor best known for his role as the serial killer Norman Bates in Alfred Hitchcock's *Psycho*)

- River Phoenix (young actor whose career was cut short by a drug overdose, he starred in notable films including *Dogfight, My Own Private Idaho, Running on Empty, Little Nikita, The Mosquito Coast*, and *Stand By Me.*)

- Sydney Pollack (actor, producer, and Academy Award–winning motion picture director. Portion of his ashes scattered along the runway at the Van Nuys Airport in Southern California.)

- Vincent Price (best remembered for his roles in low-budget horror films such as *The Fly, House on Haunted Hill, Fall of the House of Usher*, and *The Pit and the Pendulum.)*

- Johnny Ramone (guitarist for the punk rock group the Ramones)

- Christopher Reeve (actor, director, producer, and writer renowned for his film portrayal of Superman. In 1995, Reeve was rendered a quadriplegic in an equestrian accident and was confined to a wheelchair for the remainder of his life)

- Lee Remick (American actress admired for her beauty and versatility. Among her best-known films are *Anatomy of a Murder* and *Days of Wine and Roses*)

- Gene Roddenberry (the *Star Trek* creator's ashes were blasted off into space)

- Del Shannon (American rock and roller who launched into fame with his hit "Runaway" which introduced the musitron, an early form of the synthesizer. Other hits included "Hats Off to Larry," "Handy Man," "Do You Wanna Dance," and "Keep Searchin'.")

- Jay Silverheels (Canadian Mohawk Indian actor who played Tonto on the *Lone Ranger* TV series and movies including *Broken Arrow*, *Walk the Proud Arrow*, and *Alias Jesse James*.)

- Barbara Stanwyck (starring in almost a hundred films during her career, she received four nominations for the Academy Award for Best Actress: *Stella Dallas*, *Ball of Fire*, *Double Indemnity*, and *Sorry, Wrong Number*.)

- Morrie Schwartz (hero of *Tuesdays with Morrie*)

- Louis "Studs" Terkel (professional listener, talker, author, actor who requested he be cremated and have his ashes mixed with his wife's then scattered in Bughouse Square. "Scatter us there," he said. "It's against the law (so) let 'em sue us.")

- Lana Turner (nicknamed The Sweater Girl for her appearances in tight sweaters, and known for her smoldering sensuality and later for sudsy romance films with maximal glamorous evening gowns and tragedy.)

- Fats Waller (African-American jazz pianist, organist, composer, and comedic entertainer. Among his songs are "Squeeze Me," "Ain't Misbehavin'," "Blue Turning Grey Over You," "Honeysuckle Rose," "I've Got a Feeling I'm Falling," and "Jitterbug Waltz.")

- Jerry Wexler (music producer and a major record industry player who coined the term "rhythm and blues" and produced many of the biggest acts including Ray Charles, Aretha Franklin, Led Zeppelin, Wilson Pickett, Dusty Springfield, and Bob Dylan.)

- Virginia Woolf (considered one of the foremost modernist/feminist literary figures of the twentieth century, Woolf was a significant figure in London literary society and a member of the Bloomsbury Group.

Resources:

- http://www.morbid-curiosity.com/id170.htm
- Wikipedia: http://en.wikipedia.org/wiki/Main_Page
- http://www.corsinet.com/braincandy/graves.html
- http://www.corsinet.com/braincandy/dying.html
- http://www.webpanda.com/ponder/epitaphs.htm
- *Cremation in America* by Fred Rosen, Prometheus Books
- *The 2,548 Best Things Anybody Ever Said* by Robert Byrne, Fireside/Simon & Schuster
- *Purified by Fire: A History of Cremation in America* by Stephen R. Prothero, Berkeley & London : University of California Press

I am indebted to Robert Byrne and his book *The 2,548 Best Things Anybody Ever Said*—selected and compiled by the author, for many of my Quotable Quotes.

Heady Headstones, Last Gasps, and other quotable quotes were gathered from the following sources:
http://www.corsinet.com/braincandy/graves.html
www.mapping.com/words.html
www.sanftleban.com